MicroStrategy
Quick Start Guide

Data analytics and visualizations for Business Intelligence

Fernando Carlos Rivero Esqueda

BIRMINGHAM - MUMBAI

MicroStrategy Quick Start Guide

Commissioning Editor: Amey Varangaonkar
Acquisition Editor: Reshma Raman
Content Development Editor: Mohammed Yusuf Imaratwale
Technical Editor: Jinesh Topiwala
Copy Editor: Safis Editing
Project Coordinator: Hardik Bhinde
Proofreader: Safis Editing
Indexer: Priyanka Dhadke
Graphics: Jason Monteiro / Fernando Carlos Rivero Esqueda
Production Coordinator: Aparna Bhagat

First published: September 2018

Production reference: 1270918

Published by Packt Publishing Ltd.
Livery Place
35 Livery Street
Birmingham
B3 2PB, UK.

ISBN 978-1-78913-624-1

www.packtpub.com

This book is dedicated to:
My love, my wife, Talia
My smart son, Josh
My kind son, Carlos
My brave son, Samy
My friendly son, Dany
My sweet daughter, Regina
My adorable daughter, Rebeca
My supporting mom, Irma
My encouraging dad, Fernando
My reason, my God

– Fernando Carlos Rivero Esqueda

`mapt.io`

Mapt is an online digital library that gives you full access to over 5,000 books and videos, as well as industry leading tools to help you plan your personal development and advance your career. For more information, please visit our website.

Why subscribe?

- Spend less time learning and more time coding with practical eBooks and Videos from over 4,000 industry professionals

- Improve your learning with Skill Plans built especially for you

- Get a free eBook or video every month

- Mapt is fully searchable

- Copy and paste, print, and bookmark content

packt.com

Did you know that Packt offers eBook versions of every book published, with PDF and ePub files available? You can upgrade to the eBook version at `www.packt.com` and as a print book customer, you are entitled to a discount on the eBook copy. Get in touch with us at `customercare@packtpub.com` for more details.

At `www.packt.com`, you can also read a collection of free technical articles, sign up for a range of free newsletters, and receive exclusive discounts and offers on Packt books and eBooks.

Foreword

Intelligence. What does it really mean? Definitions vary from *the ability to acquire and apply knowledge and skills* to *the capacity for understanding* to *the aptitude to perceive and comprehend the meaning* of things that our mind turns into concepts. The truth is that there are as many definitions of *intelligence* as there are individuals trying to describe it. Experts have even categorized intelligence as cognitive, social, emotional, artificial, artistic, digital, business, and so on. You name it!

Truly exceptional leaders, those that are called *transformational* or *disruptive,* are considered intelligent in at least two of these categories.

I strongly believe that Fernando Rivero is part of this privileged group of transformational leaders. More than 20 years ago, I had the opportunity to recruit him as a MicroStrategy intern, pioneering business intelligence in markets struggling to understand and implement ERP systems and geographies, where BI was just a buzzword, a *nice to have,* and Decision Support Systems were perceived as a useless luxury with no clear idea of the potential benefits they might bring to companies' performance.

I witnessed Fernando's personal and professional growth for some years, as BI and DWH offerings were consolidated by the largest IT providers in the industry and transformed from BI to data mining to analytics, big data, IOT, and so on, incorporating web, mobile, and cloud computing technologies. Very few companies survived this consolidation, NASDAQ catastrophes, and other setbacks to remain faithful to their original principles and technological vision to continuously deliver innovative ways to transform data into valuable information for decision makers.

MicroStrategy Quick Start Guide is the result of Fernando's ability to explain extremely complicated ideas in a very simple way. He has transformed highly technical manuals into a *billboard for dummies,* depicting data models, dimensions, facts, attributes, metrics, and relationships as simple building blocks, understandable to any common user, and has changed the way in which business analytics should be described. He has even developed his own philosophy and manuals to instruct various attendees (consultants, power, and end users) in his MicroStrategy's training sessions.

MicroStrategy Quick Start Guide is a practical, step-by-step toolkit that will guide the reader through *the ropes to know* of this marvelous BI platform. It clarifies MicroStrategy's architecture and its powerful engine logic, covering the platform's components and information delivery channels. It addresses the MicroStrategy features that are necessary for any BI or data analytics implementation, such as design, development, visualization, connectivity, security, administration, security, and monitoring, among others, in a friendly manner.

I am confident that you will find this guide extremely useful, regardless of your level of training or expertise with MicroStrategy, and that it will be a critical factor in the success of your BI or analytics initiatives.

Juan Pablo Martinez

Former CEO, Active Data Systems

Channel Sales Manager, Informatica Mexico

I first met Fernando Rivero in 2004. Two of the people in my consulting practice at the time had been raving about their favorite professor of business intelligence at their alma mater. A short time later, by chance, that man's résumé landed on my desk. Fernando, the softly spoken professor, joined our practice and quickly became the preferred advisor to C-level executives at Fortune 500 retailers, financial services firms, and more.

Business intelligence, after all, is the science of turning the mounds of data that every company has floating around their organization into actionable information. I think of a company's data as being like the random stuff that most people have in their garage. It's not very useful in its current state. But if you can turn a random assortment of information into a way to save a company millions in expenses, or reveal a potential new line of business, then suddenly you become a very sought-after person.

Fernando was that rare consultant with deep technical mastery, along with a knack for efficiently explaining complex topics to others. In my quarter-century of leading technical consultancies, I've met few others like him.

In this book, Fernando uses the same easy-to-understand tone that made him popular with CIOs and college students alike, and reveals the essential information needed to become the resident expert in MicroStrategy business intelligence. He starts with the basics of installation and setting up your MicroStrategy work space (or *project*). Very quickly, you will be learning some of the advanced features that will capture the interest of business users, such as setting up drill maps, creating visual reports, and supporting self-service enthusiasts.

This book provides the reader with an incredibly efficient means of reaching proficiency with MicroStrategy products, and will set you on the path to being a business intelligence leader. The *lab* approach to the material keeps your hands on the keyboard to maximize your retention. It is compact, to the point, and chock full of what you need to know.

 Happy learning!

Rob Jammes

Former Professional Service Director, MicroStrategy Inc.

Professional Services Executive, Imperva

Contributors

About the author

Fernando Carlos Rivero Esqueda is a Mexican BI professional with 18 years of MicroStrategy (MSTR) experience. He earned a BS in electronic systems and two master's degrees: IT management, and an MBA from the university of Massachusetts. He is studying for an MA on Human and Family Development. He worked for 8 years for MSTR as a consultant, instructor, and educational mgr., attaining the highest possible certification: MicroStrategy Certified Engineering Principal. He taught MSTR to more than 1200 people, from consultants and directors to college students. He works now as a BI engineer for a well-known retailer in Seattle. His passion and love are his wife and kids. Fernando likes photography, piano, karate, and playing Pokémon Go with his kids. To contact him search for MBA Fernando Rivero.

I want to give thanks to God and my parents,
Irma and Fernando, for giving me the gift of life.

For understanding my long days and nights at the computer, thank you my love, Talia, and children, Josh, Carlos, Samy, Dany, Regina, and Bequis.

For your help polishing this book, thanks to my reviewers and editors, Vic, Cesar, Felipe, Yusuf, and Jinesh.

To my former managers, because without their mentoring I wouldn't be writing this book; thanks, JP, Vic, and Rob.

About the reviewers

Cesar Izazaga is a MicroStrategy expert who has worked as a business intelligence consultant over the past 10 years. Some of his clients include Intel, Visa Inc, and Rogers Communications.

His business intelligence career started back in college when he took a course taught by Fernando, where he quickly fell in love with data analysis.

He lives in Mexico with his wife and daughter and their two overactive dogs.

Victor Lozano Perales has some IT companies known as SISMEX Group since 2001; one of its focuses is BI. He is Mexican and earned his BS in Computer Science with Excellence Honors, Best in Class, from ITESM in Monterrey MX. He is a MicroStrategy Certified Developer and one of his roles at SISMEX is to lead BI the consultancy.

Prior to SISMEX's foundation, he was a software engineer for an international IT company, gaining professional and personal experience in the US, and then for one of the most important newspapers in Mexico.

He likes to help people and enjoys technology and entrepreneurship. He loves his family and enjoys watching movies with them. Exercise and good nutrition is his key, to healthy living for the love of his family and himself.

> *Thanks God for my family, who supported me in this effort, and for meeting Fer. Thank you, Fer, for your consideration. Thanks to my parents for my studies, including English lessons.*

Felipe Vilela has worked for many years with system development, and then started working in BI/DW, mainly using MicroStrategy, more than 8 years ago. He worked with many companies in Brazil and the United States, implementing MicroStrategy projects, customizing, and administrating the tool. He taught BI/DW and MicroStrategy to many companies using the company's, personal, and MicroStrategy's official courses. He also has a blog (www.vilelamstr.com). He was one of the MicroStrategy mobile app developers at MicroStrategy World 2016 and 2017. He has more than 30 MicroStrategy certifications, including the MCEP.

> *First, I would like to thank God, who is my father and savior; my wife and my son, who I love so much; my family, who are always there for me; and my friends.*

Packt is searching for authors like you

If you're interested in becoming an author for Packt, please visit `authors.packtpub.com` and apply today. We have worked with thousands of developers and tech professionals, just like you, to help them share their insight with the global tech community. You can make a general application, apply for a specific hot topic that we are recruiting an author for, or submit your own idea.

Table of Contents

Preface

Founded in 1989, MicroStrategy has been consistently recognized by Gartner as a business intelligence and analytics leader in technology. For almost 30 years, companies and organizations all over the world have trusted MicroStrategy to provide them with one of the best analytics, reporting, and mobile platforms. Nevertheless, the MicroStrategy platform can be daunting at first sight. The amount of concepts and information about MicroStrategy, combined with so many advanced features, a steep learning curve, costly courses, and limited literature, could discourage almost anyone. Moreover, the few books in the market are focused on advanced features and written for an audience with some degree of experience in business intelligence and reporting applications.

This book's objective is to help users and developers take the first step toward learning MicroStrategy by providing a good, solid foundation in a format that is easy to read and understand. The base concepts and skills learned by completing this book will aid the audience in moving to the next level in their knowledge of MicroStrategy.

Who this book is for

This book is tailored toward business and information technology professionals with little or no experience in MicroStrategy, who want to learn the basics and start building reports right away. Also, this book can be easily adopted by professionals with experience in other business intelligence reporting platforms and tools.

What this book covers

Chapter 1, *Architecture – Installing and Configuring MicroStrategy*, introduces the reader to MicroStrategy, how its technology fits into the business intelligence spectra, and how it satisfies information demands for any organization. MicroStrategy architecture is presented and explained. Client applications, such as Developer and Web, are described, as well as server components. This chapter also describes how to install the MicroStrategy Intelligence Server, as well as the client tools used to build and maintain MicroStrategy Reports and analytics objects.

Chapter 2, *Project Design – Creating Your Project Foundation*, teaches the reader about MicroStrategy Objects, specifically about Schema Objects, which are used to create an abstraction or model of an analytical database or data warehouse. These objects serve as the foundation for the MicroStrategy Project. Each object is described and explained: what it its main purpose; how to build it, in terms of what its components are; and where it can be reused.

Chapter 3, *Basic Reporting – Building Your First Reports*, introduces to the reader the Public or Application Objects and how these objects are built from Schema Objects. The first reporting objects, such as Templates, Filters, and Metrics, are described and explained. At the end of the chapter, several Report manipulations are described.

Chapter 4, *Advanced Reporting – Interacting with and Improving Your Reports*, continues to introduce new Public Objects to the reader; this time, they are objects that will allow them to step up their analysis, flexibility, and performance. Intelligent Cubes are discussed and explained as a way to publish information so that MicroStrategy reporting applications can consume it.

Chapter 5, *Dashboarding – Creating Visual Reporting*, covers visual information and dashboarding. It shows the reader how to import a data source and then create a Dashboard using Public Objects for enterprise-certified reporting, or to create a web Dashboard using self-service tools.

Chapter 6, *Security – Managing Your Users and Their Access*, introduces Configuration Objects to the reader, and covers the main security levels in MicroStrategy. Some of these objects allow administrators to set up security profiles and permissions to access objects and to create Users and Groups.

Chapter 7, *Administration – Maintaining and Monitoring your Project*, expands the knowledge about other Configuration Objects describing those which allow system administrators to perform tasks such as establishing database connectivity and scheduling data refreshes for their Reports and Intelligent Cubes. Then, the main system monitors are presented and described. Finally, three Administrative client tools are described: Object Manager, Command Manager Integrity Manager.

Appendix, *Quick Reference Tables by Object Type*, is a collection of all the quick reference tables used throughout the book by object type, for readers to reference.

To get the most out of this book

This book requires a general understanding of application software and common graphical user interface applications, such as Windows Explorer. In addition, it is assumed that the reader understands basic business intelligence concepts and database terminology (tables, columns, fields, rows, and so on).

A PC with a Windows 64-bit operating system is required. Also, to get the most out of all the exercises, the following software should be installed (in addition to MicroStrategy):

- Microsoft .NET Framework 4.0 or higher
- Internet Explorer or Google Chrome
- Internet Information Services (IIS 10 or higher)
- Microsoft Access (2007 or newer)

For a detailed list of system requirements, you can check `https://microstrategyhelp.` `atlassian.net/wiki/spaces/README104/pages/38305888/MicroStrategy+10.` `4+System+Requirements.`

Download the example code files

You can download the example file for this book from your account at `www.packt.com`. If you purchased this book elsewhere, you can visit `www.packt.com/support` and register to have the files emailed directly to you.

You can download the file by following these steps:

1. Log in or register at `www.packt.com`.
2. Select the **SUPPORT** tab.
3. Click on **Code Downloads & Errata**.
4. Enter the name of the book in the **Search** box and follow the onscreen instructions.

Once the file is downloaded, please make sure that you unzip or extract the folder using the latest version of:

- WinRAR/7-Zip for Windows
- Zipeg/iZip/UnRarX for Mac
- 7-Zip/PeaZip for Linux

The example file for the book is also hosted on GitHub at `https://github.com/PacktPublishing/MicroStrategy-Quick-Start-Guide`. In case there's an update to the file, it will be updated on the existing GitHub repository.

We also have other code bundles from our rich catalog of books and videos available at `https://github.com/PacktPublishing/`. Check them out!

Download the color images

We also provide a PDF file that has color images of the screenshots/diagrams used in this book. You can download it here: `http://www.packtpub.com/sites/default/files/downloads/9781789136241_ColorImages.pdf`.

Conventions used

There are a number of text conventions used throughout this book.

`CodeInText`: Indicates code words in text, database table names, folder names, filenames, file extensions, pathnames, dummy URLs, user input, and Twitter handles. Here is an example: "The Template will determine the `SELECT/FROM` clause in the SQL that MicroStrategy sends to the database, whereas the attribute IDs determine `GROUP BY`."

Bold: Indicates a new term, an important word, or words that you see onscreen. For example, words in menus or dialog boxes appear in the text like this. Here is an example: "Go to the **Schema** menu | **Update Schema**."

Warnings or important notes appear like this.

Tips and tricks appear like this.

Get in touch

Feedback from our readers is always welcome.

General feedback: If you have questions about any aspect of this book, mention the book title in the subject of your message and email us at customercare@packt.com.

Errata: Although we have taken every care to ensure the accuracy of our content, mistakes do happen. If you have found a mistake in this book, we would be grateful if you would report this to us. Please visit www.packt.com/submit-errata, selecting your book, clicking on the Errata Submission Form link, and entering the details.

Piracy: If you come across any illegal copies of our works in any form on the Internet, we would be grateful if you would provide us with the location address or website name. Please contact us at copyright@packt.com with a link to the material.

If you are interested in becoming an author: If there is a topic that you have expertise in and you are interested in either writing or contributing to a book, please visit authors.packt.com.

Reviews

Please leave a review. Once you have read and used this book, why not leave a review on the site that you purchased it from? Potential readers can then see and use your unbiased opinion to make purchase decisions, we at Packt can understand what you think about our products, and our authors can see your feedback on their book. Thank you!

For more information about Packt, please visit packt.com.

Architecture - Installing and Configuring MicroStrategy

1

There are a good number of solutions, tools, and software that help companies and organizations to make sense of their data by turning it into information. This information needs to be analyzed and visualized in such a way that it can generate knowledge and insight into the past, present, and future of the organization. This cycle of data-information-knowledge-action is commonly known as business intelligence or business analytics, depending on the usage of that knowledge and the focus and perspective of those who make decisions. In simple terms, we can think of business intelligence as a way to maintain and optimize the present by looking into the past, whereas business analytics focuses on transforming the future by changing the present. MicroStrategy has been one of the market's leading business intelligence and analytics platforms since 1989.

This first chapter will introduce the MicroStrategy platform and explain its main components. Then it will cover MicroStrategy installation and configuration so that readers can start creating their first project and reporting applications right away. The following topics will be covered:

- MicroStrategy architecture
- Intelligence Server engines description
- Intelligence Server components description
- Web and mobile server description
- Client applications for developers
- Client applications for administrators
- Client applications for information delivery
- Installation and configuration
- The MicroStrategy metadata
- Creating and configuring project sources

MicroStrategy architecture

MicroStrategy is a platform suite which satisfies both **Business intelligence** (**BI**) and **Business Analytics** (**BA**) needs within an organization. It features powerful application software capable of resolving any question related to the past, present, or future of a given company, making MicroStrategy one of the best platforms for BI and BA in the market. MicroStrategy is capable of covering all BI/BA styles from basic reporting, OLAP business analysis, scorecards and dashboards, to more sophisticated predictive analytics and data mining.

MicroStrategy is a hybrid online analytical processing platform, also known as HOLAP. It is capable of generating queries or a **SQL** (**Structured Query Language**) from virtually any major relational database, such as Oracle, Teradata, Redshift, SQL Server, and so on. This is what gives MicroStrategy its ROLAP (relational online analytical processing) capabilities. However, it could also work as a MOLAP (multidimensional online analytical processing) with the use of cube structures.

As a developer, it is important to understand MicroStrategy's architecture. The following diagram depicts how MicroStrategy's components commonly fit into the big picture of BI/BA within an organization:

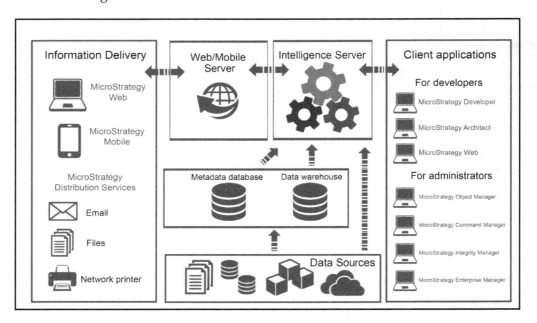

Microstrategy's architecture

At MicroStrategy's platform core resides the Intelligence Server, which connects to a data layer. This data layer acts as a data source, and it could be a relational database with enterprise data, such as a data warehouse or a specialized data mart. However, the Intelligence Server can also connect to a nonrelational data source such as transactional applications (OLTP), flat files, cube data structures, and website content, to name a few. There is also a metadata database or repository that the Intelligence Server uses to store the definitions of all MicroStrategy objects.

There are three main groups of client applications, or tools, within the MicroStrategy suite. First, there are client applications, which allow developers to create reporting and analytics solutions. These applications are MicroStrategy Developer, MicroStrategy Architect and MicroStrategy Web. Next, the information is delivered to the final user or analyst via MicroStrategy Mobile, MicroStrategy Web, Email, Printer, or File (using MicroStrategy Distribution Services, Narrowcast Server, or MicroStrategy Office). Finally, there are some applications with the purpose of managing and monitoring the business intelligence projects. Some examples are MicroStrategy Object Manager, MicroStrategy Command Manager, MicroStrategy Enterprise Manager, and MicroStrategy Integrity Manager.

 Narrowcast Server is an information delivery application that is being replaced by Distribution Services.

In the following sections, you will learn in detail how each component fits into the whole architecture, resulting in a robust business intelligence and analytics platform.

Main server components

There are two main server groups in the MicroStrategy architecture. The core of the MicroStrategy platform is an application server called Intelligence Server. There are also two servers that will publish the information to the appropriate delivery method. These servers are the Web and Mobile servers. In the following sections we will learn about them.

The MicroStrategy Intelligence Server

The following diagram shows where the Intelligence Server resides within the platform's architecture:

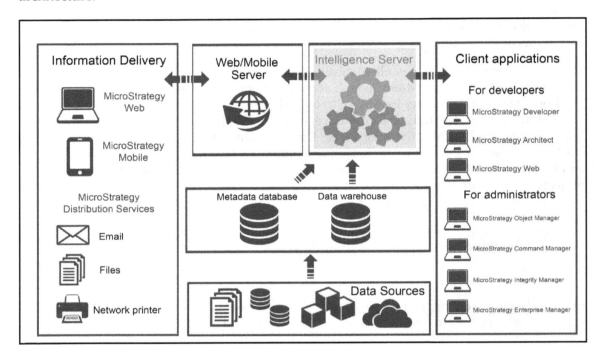

The application server responsible for orchestrating every other component in the MicroStrategy platform is the Intelligence Server, also called I-Server. It is also the component that handles communication with the data sources (such as data warehouse or nonrelational databases) and the metadata database. There are three main I-Server engines, shown as follows:

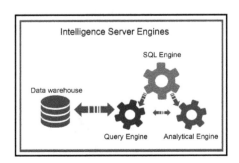

- **SQL Engine**
  The SQL Engine is responsible for creating the optimized SQL for the database. Once the SQL is generated, the I-Server SQL Engine will pass it to the Query Engine for execution. The SQL Engine also controls the other two engines.

- **Query Engine**
  The Query Engine is responsible for sending the SQL towards the database. The I-Server Query Engine will connect to the database via ODBC (Open Database Connectivity) and execute the query. Once the SQL is executed, it will receive it and send it to the Analytical Engine for cross tabbing or additional nonSQL functions.

- **Analytical Engine**
  The Analytical Engine is responsible for nonSQL actions such as in-memory manipulations and cross tabbing. Some typical examples of calculations not resolved by the SQL are functions that are not commonly supported by the database like rankings, subtotals, and other OLAP functions. This engine is also responsible for laying out the data in a cross-tab format. Finally, the Analytical Engine is in charge of any in-memory manipulation of the report (this is after the dataset is returned from the database) such as pivoting, Page-by, sorting, and conditional formatting.

In addition, there are three I-Server components that allow scalability, optimization, and distribution of the information:

- **OLAP Services**
  MicroStrategy OLAP Services enable MOLAP capabilities with the creation and manipulation of in-memory datasets called Intelligent Cubes. (For more information refer to `Chapter 4`, *Advanced Reporting - Interacting with and Improving Your Reports*).

- **Report Services**
  MicroStrategy Report Services allow flexible reporting layouts to create dashboards and scorecards. (For more information refer to `Chapter 5`, *Dashboarding - Creating Visual Reporting*).

- **Distribution Services**
  MicroStrategy Distribution Services facilitate the delivery of reports and dashboards supporting multiple formats, schedules, and transmitters such as email, printers, and file servers.

MicroStrategy Web and Mobile servers

The following diagram shows where Web and Mobile servers reside within the platform's architecture:

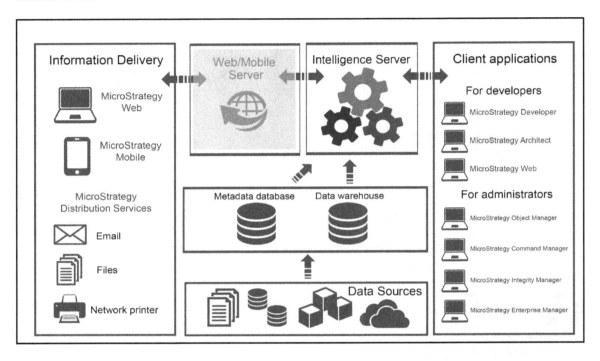

Apart from the Intelligence Server, there are other two server components that connect to the information delivery face of the architecture. These servers are MicroStrategy Web and Mobile. The software components of MicroStrategy Web and Mobile are deployed and published using a web server such as Tomcat or IIS. These two communicate with the MicroStrategy Intelligence Server in order to deliver information to the corresponding Web and Mobile client counterparts.

Client applications

The MicroStrategy platform provides a complete set of client tools and applications that enable developers to build and design BI and analytics solutions, administrators to manage BI projects and their life cycle, and users to interact with data, and to discover and analyze it correspondingly.

All these client applications connect to the Intelligence Server, which manages them and controls how, when, and where the data and information should be directed.

For developers

The following diagram shows where developer tools reside within the platform's architecture:

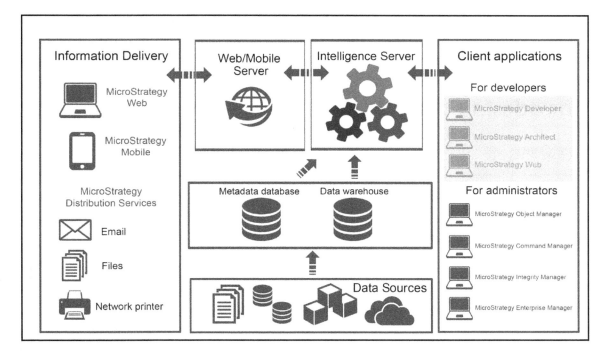

The first client tools are the ones used for design and developing. The applications are MicroStrategy Developer, MicroStrategy Architect, and MicroStrategy Web:

- **MicroStrategy Developer**
  Formerly known as MicroStrategy Desktop, MicroStrategy Developer is an application that gives developers the ability to create reporting and analytics solutions. This is the tool that power users or advanced developers utilize to build Public Objects, which include Reports, Metrics, Filters, and dashboards. MicroStrategy Developer also contains administrative features to configure, monitor, and secure the BI project.

- **MicroStrategy Architect**
  MicroStrategy Architect is embedded into MicroStrategy Developer's interface and enables designers and developers to create objects that map to the database structures. These objects are called schema objects. (For more information refer to `Chapter 2`, *Project Design - Creating Your Project Foundation*).

- **MicroStrategy Web**
  MicroStrategy Web is a light client application that permits both developing and performing interactive analysis. It provides a wide range of options, from data browsing, report manipulation and dashboard creation, to self-service, information distribution, and data discovery. In some, this client is used by both developers and final users as well.

For administrators

The following diagram shows where administrator tools reside within the platform's architecture:

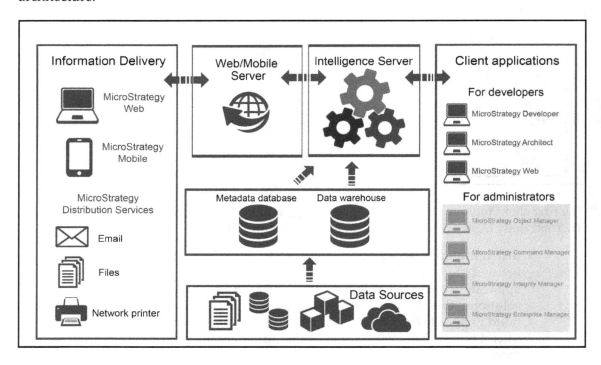

The second set of client components includes those used for administration, script automation, monitoring, and managing the BI life cycle. Some applications are MicroStrategy Object Manager, MicroStrategy Command Manager, MicroStrategy Enterprise Manager and MicroStrategy Integrity Manager:

- **MicroStrategy Object Manager**
  MicroStrategy Object Manager allows administrators to copy or promote objects across different environments such as nonproduction, test, and production.

- **MicroStrategy Command Manager**
  MicroStrategy Command Manager gives the administrators the ability to create scripts to automate the most common administrative tasks. Third-party applications such as BMC Control-M and Airflow, can be integrated with MicroStrategy using Command Manager.

- **MicroStrategy Enterprise Manager**
  MicroStrategy Enterprise Manager enables analysis of the information generated by the Intelligence Server and the project's usage. It provides a set of Reports and Dashboards that allow administrators to monitor system and report usage, as well as statistics that can be leveraged to create strategies to optimize the BI and analytics environment.

- **MicroStrategy Integrity Manager**
  MicroStrategy Integrity Manager gives developers a tool to compare environments and the objects within, identifying and highlighting changes or differences that could occur between development, test, and/or production environments.

For users and analysts

The following diagram shows where information delivery tools reside within the platform's architecture:

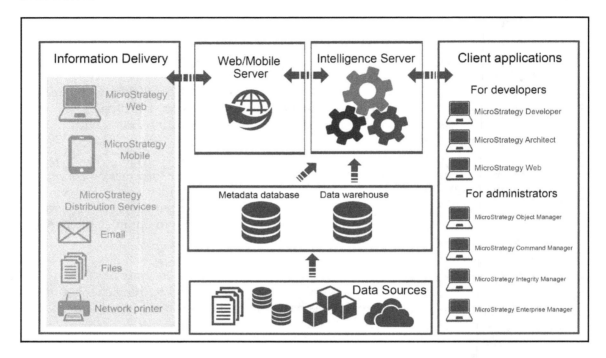

The third set of client applications includes the ones that deliver the information to the final users and analysts. These clients are MicroStrategy Web, MicroStrategy Mobile, and MicroStrategy Distribution Services:

- **MicroStrategy Web**
  MicroStrategy Web not only serves as software for development but also as a web-based client that delivers rich visualizations, powerful report manipulations, and interactive dashboards. MicroStrategy Web is integrated with MicroStrategy Distribution Services to deliver information in a variety of formats and media, such as email, files, or printed material.

- **MicroStrategy Mobile**
  MicroStrategy Mobile delivers reports and dashboards anytime and anywhere to tablets and phones such as iPads, iPhones, and Android phones and tablets. MicroStrategy Mobile is fully integrated with the MicroStrategy platform, which allows it to use its report manipulation and visualization features, its flexibility, and at the same time provide security and scalability.
- **MicroStrategy Distribution Services**
  MicroStrategy Distribution Services is the component of MicroStrategy Intelligence Server that performs the delivery of reports and dashboards in a full range of methods or locations (email, files, MicroStrategy history lists, or network printers) and formats (Excel, PDF, HTML, CSV, text, and so on).

Installation and configuration

The information conveyed in this section provides the prerequisites and minimum system requirements to install the current MicroStrategy, version 10.X. For prior versions, similar prerequisites apply. To make sure the requirements are met, check the MicroStrategy *Release Notes* (`Readme` file) that are included with the packaged installation files. In addition, MicroStrategy Online Community (`https://community.microstrategy.com/s/`) is a great place to find documentation, forums and the latest information about MicroStrategy.

Prerequisites

Before installing the MicroStrategy suite you must make sure these prerequisites are covered:

- MicroStrategy installation files: Typically downloaded from the MicroStrategy download site in a compressed file.
- License Key: Obtained from MicroStrategy account executive. MicroStrategy can also be downloaded and installed on a 30-day free trial.
- Administrative privileges: On a Windows installation it is necessary to have a domain account with administrative privileges and access is required. For Unix/Linux, root access is necessary.

Required software:

- For Windows:
  - Microsoft .NET Framework 4.0 or 4.5
  - Web server (to support MicroStrategy Web on ASP.NET) Microsoft Internet Information Services 7.x-8.x
- For Linux/Unix:
  - Web server (to support MicroStrategy Web on J2EE) such as Oracle WebLogic 12c or 10.3.x, IBM WebSphere 7.x-8.0.X, or Apache Tomcat 6.0.x-7.0.X

System requirements

The following table serves as a guideline for the MicroStrategy 10 platform installation. These include recommended memory, available storage, and processor for each component.

MicroStrategy component	Minimum memory	Storage	Hardware
MicroStrategy Intelligence Server	4 GB	12 GB (as a rule, memory times 3)	Windows: 64-bit
MicroStrategy Web (Server)	4 GB	0.5 GB	Windows: 64-bit
MicroStrategy Mobile (Server)	4 GB	0.5 GB	Windows: 64-bit
MicroStrategy Developer (including Architect)	2 GB	0.25 GB	Windows: 64-bit or 32-bit
MicroStrategy Object Manager	1 GB	0.25 GB	Windows: 64-bit or 32-bit
MicroStrategy Command Manager	2 GB	0.25 GB	Windows: 64-bit or 32-bit
MicroStrategy Enterprise Manager	1 GB	0.25 GB	Windows: 64-bit
MicroStrategy Integrity Manager	2 GB	0.25 GB	Windows: 64-bit

Notes:

For Linux/Unix the recommended hardware is:

- Oracle SPARC
- IBM AIX Power Architecture
- HP-UX Intel Itanium
- Red Hat/SUSE Linux 32- and 64-bit

For a complete list of supported and certified configurations, you can google MicroStrategy certified and supported configurations. With every release, MicroStrategy Inc. publishes detailed information about system requirements and supported configurations. The current one can be found at: `https://www2.microstrategy.com/producthelp/10.10/Readme/content/certified_configurations.htm`.

Windows installation

To install MicroStrategy on a Windows machine, it is necessary to log in to the workstation or server using an account with administrative privileges. In addition, the database servers must be in reach (via ODBC/JDBC) from the Intelligent Server to guarantee connectivity to the data warehouse (or data marts) and metadata database.

> For development and production installations it is strongly recommended to install the Web/Mobile component on a separate machine from the Intelligent Server. Same goes for other client tools such as Enterprise Manager, Object Manager, Command Manager and Integrity Manager, it is recommended to have them installed on a separate machine too.

The installation of MicroStrategy is simple and guided by the installation wizard:

1. Download the MicroStrategy suite.

   - For licensed customers go to the MicroStrategy download site: `http://download.microstrategy.com`.
   - There is also a free 30-day trial available at: `https://www.microstrategy.com/us/get-started/enterprise-evaluation`.

2. Locate and execute the setup file (`MICROSTRATEGY.exe`), shown as follows:

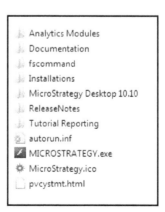

3. This action will launch the installation wizard.

4. Review and accept the license agreement and input the **License Key**, shown as follows:

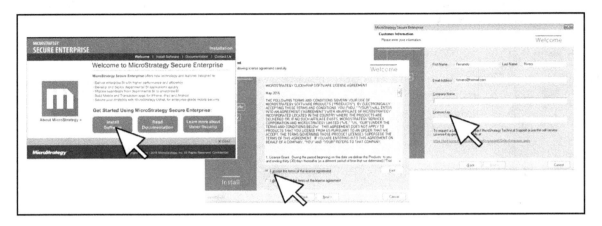

Licences agreement and Licences Key

5. Install options, including destination location and how many products in the suite will be installed, as shown in the next screenshot:

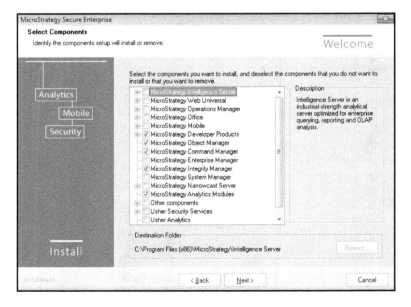

Lists of the products in the suite that will be installed

6. If MicroStrategy Web is selected, it is necessary to establish the **Internet Information Services** (**IIS**) virtual directory in which the MicroStrategy Web code (ASP.NET) will be deployed. Similarly, for MicroStrategy Mobile, a new virtual directory for the IIS will be created.

7. Continue with the summary of products to be installed and start the process.

8. When the installation wizard completes, restart the computer to make sure the installation process has completed successfully.

Unix/Linux installation

There are different installation methods for MicroStrategy on Unix/Linux, either using a **Graphical User Interface** (**GUI**), in command-line mode, or silent mode (automated). The GUI mode and the command-line mode will launch the MicroStrategy Installation Wizard displaying the same pages and requesting the same information as the Windows counterpart. It is important to note, though, that MicroStrategy Object Manager , MicroStrategy Developer and MicroStrategy Enterprise Manager can't be installed in a Unix/Linux box.

The MicroStrategy metadata

By definition, a metadata is "data about the data." It is usually a file or database that describes another set of data or information. In MicroStrategy, the metadata repository is a database that contains the definitions of database objects such as tables and fields in a way that developers and users can easily understand. The MicroStrategy metadata could be thought of as a logical bridge between the technicalities of the database and the business terms, measures, and contexts of the organization.

The MicroStrategy metadata maps logical abstractions, called objects, to physical database objects, as illustrated in the following diagram:

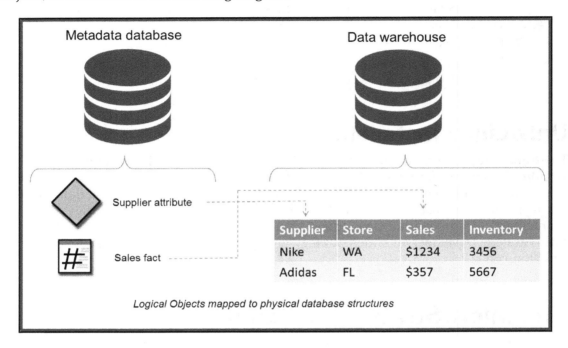

Logical Objects mapped to physical database structures

Creating and configuring MicroStrategy metadata

Before creating the MicroStrategy metadata, it is necessary to have the following two prerequisites ready:

- A blank database (Amazon Redshift, DB2, Informix, Impala, SQL Server, Oracle, and so on. For a complete list of certified MicroStrategy metadata databases, check the Readme file or release notes corresponding to the version you are installing.)
- A DSN (Data Source Name) using the corresponding ODBC/JDBC driver to that blank database.

MicroStrategy Connectivity Wizard can also be used to create a DSN.

The steps to create the MicroStrategy metadata are:

1. Open the MicroStrategy **Configuration Wizard** (`macfgwizw.EXE`). This tool will let you create a MicroStrategy metadata, configure an Intelligence Server, and create a project source among other configuration tasks, as shown in the following screenshots:

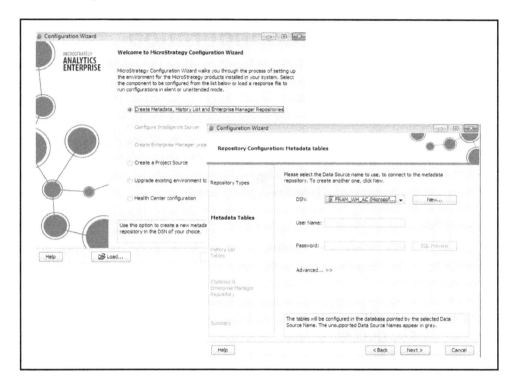

2. Select the corresponding option for metadata creation: | **Create Metadata, History List and Enterprise Manager Repositories**.
3. Select a **DSN**. The DSN will have the connectivity information and driver to access the blank database using ODBC/JDBC protocol.
4. Follow the review window and click **Next** until the metadata table creation starts.

5. During the creation of the MicroStrategy metadata, the MicroStrategy **Configuration Wizard** creates an empty shell with table structures that will host data about the data. The data that will be later populated within the structures is what we will refer to as MicroStrategy objects. This concept will be explained in the next chapter.

Intelligence Server configuration

Once the Intelligence Server is installed, it needs to be pointed to a MicroStrategy metadata. Once again the **Configuration Wizard** is used to perform this task. The object resulting from configuring an Intelligence Server is called a Server Definition. In order to create one, it is necessary to take into consideration the following prerequisites:

- The **Configuration Wizard** must be executed directly from the same machine where the Intelligence Server is running
- A DSN pointed to the MicroStrategy metadata database must be created in the same machine where the Intelligence Server is running

The steps to configure an Intelligence Server, pointing it to a MicroStrategy metadata are:

1. Launch the MicroStrategy **Configuration Wizard** (if you proceed from the above procedure, the MicroStrategy metadata creation, this wizard should be already open for you).
2. Select the corresponding option for the Intelligence Server configuration: | **Configure Intelligence Server.**
3. Select a **DSN**. This DSN must point to the metadata.
4. Once the DSN information is entered, it is necessary to either create or select an existing Server Definition.
5. The configuration process begins with the Intelligence Server being stopped, then it is pointed to the specified metadata and automatically started again, completing the Server Definition creation or switching to a different one.

Project sources (2-tier and 3-tier)

Once the MicroStrategy metadata is built and the Intelligence Server configured, it is necessary to create one or more Project Sources. A Project Source could be defined as a direct or indirect access point to the metadata. It is used by MicroStrategy Developer and other client interfaces to build, interact, and manage the contents of the MicroStrategy metadata. A Project Source can be created using the MicroStrategy **Configuration Wizard** or the **Project Source Manager**.

There are two types of Project Sources:

- **2-Tier (Direct)**: It is a Project Source pointed directly to a MicroStrategy metadata using an ODBC/DSN connection. This type of configuration is not recommended for production implementation since it won't guarantee mutual exclusion to the metadata. The 2-Tier configuration, illustrated in the following diagram, is only recommended for some maintenance and administrative tasks that require exclusive access to the metadata while the Intelligence Server is down.

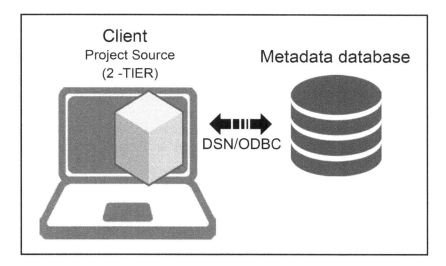

To create a 2-Tier or Direct project source it is necessary to have a DSN/ODBC connection ready pointing to the MicroStrategy metadata database and corresponding credentials. Following are steps to create it from Developer:

1. **Tools Menu | Project Source Manager.**
2. Provide a Project Source name.
3. **Add |** select in connection mode **Direct.**
4. Provide ODBC DSN with corresponding login and password.

The following screenshot shows what your Project Source Manager will look like:

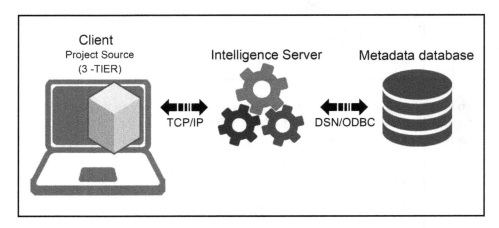

- **3-Tier (server)**: This is a Project Source pointed to the MicroStrategy Intelligence Server that in turns points to the MicroStrategy metadata. This is the configuration used for development and production. A 3-Tier configuration will guarantee that the access to the MicroStrategy metadata is controlled by the Intelligence Server providing centralization, security and fail over support (when combined with a cluster of servers). The below diagram depicts a 3-tier configuration:

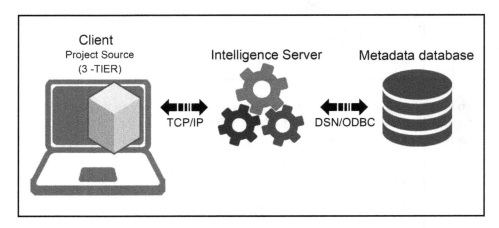

To create a 3-Tier or server Project Source, it is necessary to have the Intelligence Server IP address or server name. Follow these steps to create it from MicroStrategy Developer:

1. Go to **Tools Menu** | **Project Source Manager.**
2. Provide a Project Source name.
3. **Add** | select in connection mode **Server.**
4. Provide the Intelligence Server IP address, or server name, and a port number if applicable.

4-Tier configuration (MicroStrategy Web and/or Mobile)

Once the Intelligence Server is configured and pointed to a MicroStrategy metadata, the MicroStrategy Web and/or Mobile Server should be configured as well. Open the Web Administrator page, it is usually found in this URL if installed on Internet Information Services (IIS) Web Server `https://<your server name>/asp/Admin.aspx`. Then add the Intelligence Server IP address or domain name to connect via TCP/IP. The following diagram depicts this type of arrangement, which is called 4-Tier configuration:

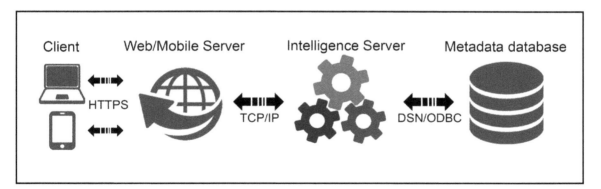

Summary

At this point, you should be familiar with the MicroStrategy Platform architecture and understand how the different components relate to each other. Also, you should be able to install MicroStrategy and perform basic configurations such as metadata database creation, Intelligence Server configuration, and Project Source creation (in 2 and 3-Tiers).

The next chapter will introduce the important concept of MicroStrategy Objects. We will learn about a specific category, which will be the foundation for any MicroStrategy Project: The Schema Objects.

2
Project Design - Creating Your Project Foundation

Technically speaking, MicroStrategy's core task is to translate business questions into the language that databases speak: SQL. In other words, MicroStrategy offers a logical bridge between business users and the data. This bridge is possible because of MicroStrategy's Objects, which in turn reside in its metadata database.

This chapter will establish the base for designing and building a MicroStrategy project. It will first define and explain the concept of MicroStrategy Objects and then describe the main object categories. Then the main Schema Objects, such as Attributes and Facts, will be covered. The following topics will be the focus of this chapter:

- What is a MicroStrategy Object?
- Which are the main object categories?
- Understanding a MicroStrategy Project and how to create one
- Understanding a MicroStrategy Schema Object
- Explaining MicroStrategy Attributes and how to create one
- Explaining MicroStrategy Facts and how to create one
- Explaining MicroStrategy Hierarchies and how to create one
- Explaining MicroStrategy Transformations and how to create one

MicroStrategy Objects

MicroStrategy Objects are logical abstractions of mainly database components, such as tables and columns. However, there are some objects that represent other things such as databases (connections), users, server nodes, schedules, and devices, to mention a few. All MicroStrategy Objects are stored in the MicroStrategy metadata database. In other words, if it is stored in the metadata then it must be a MicroStrategy Object.

This wide variety of MicroStrategy Objects are grouped into the following three main categories:

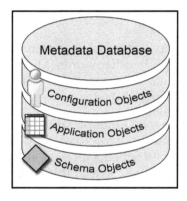

Three categories of Microstrategy

- **Schema Objects**: These objects directly represent database objects such as columns, tables, and partitions. Some examples are: Tables, Attributes, Facts, Hierarchies, and Transformations.
- **Application Objects**: Also known as Public Objects, these objects represent reporting and visualization objects. Some examples are: Reports, Templates, Metrics, Filters, Prompts, and Documents.
- **Configuration Objects**: These objects represent administration, security, and Configuration Objects. Some examples are: Users, Groups, Database Connections, and Schedules.

Framework to learn about MicroStrategy Objects

Some years ago, when I used to teach MicroStrategy, I utilized a very effective framework to learn about the multiple and diverse MicroStrategy Objects. This framework consists of three simple questions:

• What is it for?	Describe the purpose of the MicroStrategy Object.
• What is it made of?	List what other MicroStrategy Objects reside within (its components) or what it represents.
• Where can it be used?	Explain in which other MicroStrategy Objects it could be embedded (its dependents).

I will use this same framework for each MicroStrategy Object covered in this book.

MicroStrategy Analytics Modules

When MicroStrategy is installed, there is the option to install MicroStrategy Analytics Modules. Basically, this option will install two sample projects: MicroStrategy Tutorial and Human Resources Analysis Module. These two projects are installed and configured automatically. Both the data warehouse and the metadata databases reside on Microsoft Access. In addition, a 2-Tier Project Source is also created and accessible from MicroStrategy Developer. The login is *Administrator* with a blank password.

It is recommended to leave these sample projects to perform testing of MicroStrategy Features and self-training in a DEV or System Test environments, never in Production. Otherwise, these could be uninstalled. Throughout this book, we will use these two projects to describe examples and perform exercises.

MicroStrategy Developer

MicroStrategy Developer is a client interface that was conceived while thinking of an interface that the majority of the developers and users are familiar with: Windows Explorer. Microsoft Windows Explorer is a tool that helps the user to visualize, manage, organize, create, and delete files in a PC. Similarly, MicroStrategy Developer (which by the way was called MicroStrategy Desktop for many years before version 9.5) is a tool that helps the user to visualize, manage, organize, create, and delete MicroStrategy Objects in the metadata.

Although other MicroStrategy clients, covered in `Chapter 1`, *Architecture – Installing and Configuring MicroStrategy*, will offer some specific functionality and interaction with the MicroStrategy Objects, MicroStrategy Developer is the main client to develop and manage all three object categories, as shown in the following screenshot:

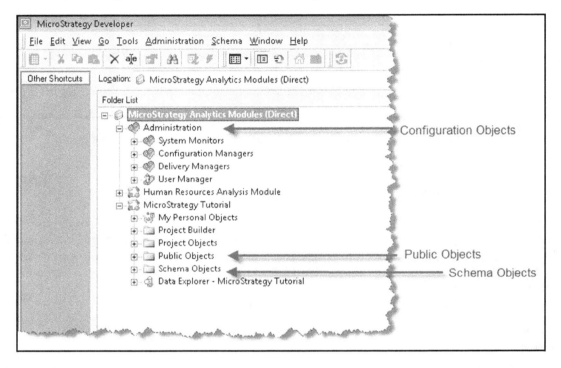

Using MicroStrategy Developer to manage all three categories

Notice that the MicroStrategy Developer tree structure is similar to that of Windows Explorer. Similarly, actions such as drag and drop, copy and paste, renaming (F2), and folder creation, to name a few, follow the same paradigm as in Windows, making MicroStrategy Developer very familiar and intuitive to the developer and user. Although there are some folders already created by default by MicroStrategy, developers can create as many as they want, rename them, and move Schema and Public Objects arbitrarily within these. However, it is recommended to keep these objects separated for ease of administration and maintenance. Conversely, the configuration objects only reside within the section named **Administration**.

MicroStrategy Projects

MicroStrategy Projects are Configuration Objects, which group all other objects within (Public and Schema). The following is a quick reference table for this MicroStrategy Object:

	1) What is it for?	To contain other objects grouped by business affinity
	2) What is it made of?	All Public and Schema Objects
	3) Where can it be used?	N/a. This is the "largest" object in the metadata

The Projects are usually created according to a business area (such as marketing, finance, and human resources) or, in some organizations, by the technology that supports its data source (such as Teradata, Oracle, SQL Server). In any case, a MicroStrategy Project helps developers and users to organize their reporting and analytics applications. There are other Configuration Objects, but these will be covered in Chapter 6, *Security – Managing Your Users and Their Access* and Chapter 7, *Administration – Maintaining and Monitoring Your Project*.

Project structure

When a MicroStrategy Project is created, a general folder structure common to every project is generated:

- **My Personal Objects**: This set of folders is meant to save objects that are not shared among other users. Meaning, whatever is saved within it remains private to the logged-in user (and the MicroStrategy Administrator).
- **Project Builder**: Project Builder is a wizard to create quick projects and proof of concepts. This folder within the project structure will hold the created objects resulting from the process.
- **Project Objects**: This folder holds some specific Application / Public Objects such as Security Filters and Subtotals.
- **Public Objects**: This folder stores the remaining Application Objects generally available to users and is shared among them.

- **Schema Objects**: This folder contains Schema Objects created by the project Architect.
- **Data explorer**: This is a data visualization tree that will show the Project's Attributes and their relationship along with the elements (data) stored in the dimension or lookup tables.

This structure provides a guide for developers to store the different objects and publish them for final users. It is also best practice to use this default folder structure. However, they are free to rename and move the objects to whichever location they want. There are only a few locations that are mandatory for some specific actions and/or functionality. These locations are:

- **Public Objects / Reports**: This location is mapped to MicroStrategy Web as a `Shared Reports` folder. The objects and subfolders within are visible through the Web Client interface.
- **Schema Objects / Hierarchies / Data Explorer**: This folder contains Hierarchies that the developer wants to make available through the Data Explorer visualization tree. We will learn about Hierarchies later in this chapter.

Exercise – create your first Project

In this exercise, you will use the MicroStrategy Project Creation Assistant to create and configure your first Project:

1. Log into the **MicroStrategy Analytics Modules (Direct)** Project Source. Use as credentials Administrator/no password.
2. Go to the **Menu Schema | Create New Project**.
3. The **Project Creation Assistant** will open. Select **Create project** and add the `MicroStrategy Essentials` name and a description (optional). Then click **OK**, as shown in the following screenshot:

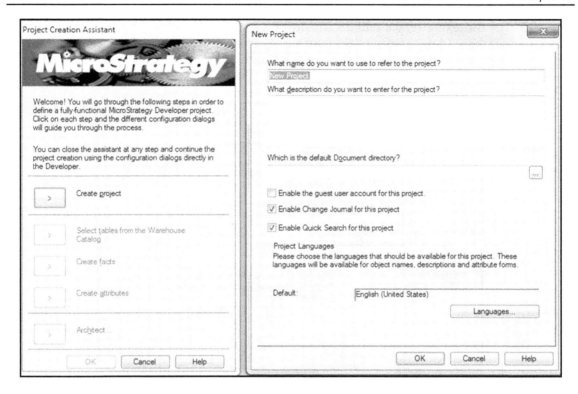

Project Creation Assistant

4. The Project is created and the user can continue using the wizard, or exit by clicking **OK** and follow the project configuration and objects creation manually.

5. For this exercise, we will do an additional step that will help to associate a database (data warehouse) to our newly created project. Click on **Select tables from the Warehouse Catalog**. This action will prompt the selection of a **Database Instance**, shown as follows:

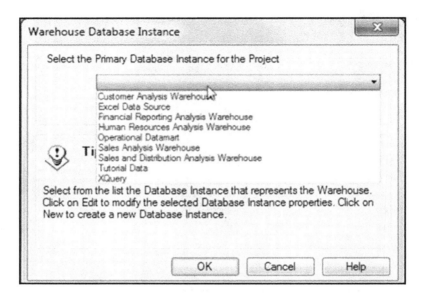

Associating a database to our newly created project

6. Select **Tutorial Data**. A MicroStrategy **Database Instance** is a configuration object used to connect to a database. We will learn later in Chapter 7, *Administration – Maintaining and Monitoring Your Project*, how to create them and configure a MicroStrategy Project, pointing it to a data warehouse or data mart. For the sake of this exercise, we will use a previously created Database Instance pointing to a retailer called Tutorial. If you want to see the Microsoft Access database, it is located within the Tutorial Reporting folder (in Windows C:\Program Files (x86)\MicroStrategy\Tutorial Reporting) with the name TUTORIAL_DATA_7200.mdb.

 Unix/Linux installations don't have this Microsoft Access file.

7. When you click **OK**, the **Warehouse Catalog** is opened. We will later explain what this is. For this exercise, just close the window (red X on right corner). Then again click **OK** on the **Project Creation Assistant**. You will see a message telling you that it is possible to continue the Project creation without the assistant. Don't click **OK** again.

8. This finalizes the exercise. You should now see your new Project within the Project Source along with the **MicroStrategy Tutorial** and **Human Resources Analysis Module** Projects.

Your building blocks – Schema Objects

The MicroStrategy Schema Objects are going to be the foundation of any project. These objects serve as building blocks on which other objects will be erected. Generally speaking, Schema Objects are mapped to database structures such as tables or columns with a few exceptions in which other Schema Objects are used as part of their components. Usually, there is only one person at a time creating or modifying Schema Objects. This person is called the project Architect. It is not recommended to have multiple persons modifying Schema Objects since this could lead to metadata inconsistencies and eventually corruption. Once any change has been performed to a schema object, it is necessary to **commit** this change into the metadata. To do so the Architect must **Update Schema**.

Exercise – updating Schema

It is very important to update the project's Schema every time there is a Schema Object change, addition, or deletion. In this exercise, you will learn how to update the Schema with the following steps:

1. Select the project where the schema will be updated. For this exercise select the **MicroStrategy Tutorial** project.
2. Open the project by double clicking on it or clicking on the plus symbol on its left.
3. Go to the **Schema** menu | **Update Schema**.

4. On the next window, shown as follows, make sure only the first option is selected with **Update schema logical information** | **Update**:

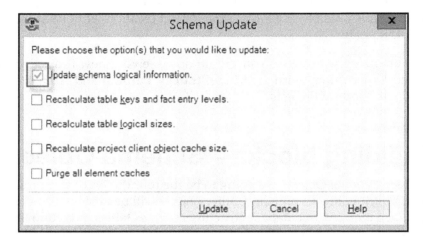

Selecting the Update Schema logical information

The other options are related to other Schema and administrative tasks.

5. This finalizes the exercise.

The schema can be updated at any time, even if no change has been introduced on the Schema Objects (like in the exercise). However, it is mandatory to do so when any schema object has been modified, created, or deleted. Failing to update the schema might result in memory differences with the physical metadata and eventually a metadata corruption.

The Source – Tables

The first **Schema Object** to be created must be a MicroStrategy Table. The following is a quick reference table for this MicroStrategy Object:

	1) What is it for?	To map fields to a physical table or view in a database. To create MicroStrategy expressions
	2) What is it made of?	Columns and data types
	3) Where can it be used?	Attributes, Facts and Transformations

This object is simply the logical representation of a table in the database (data warehouse). MicroStrategy imports into the object definition the table name, structure, columns, and data types. In addition, MicroStrategy assigns a value to the table based on the fields and Attributes mapped to it. It is important to mention that this number doesn't represent a measure of megabytes or number of rows but instead a conceptual value; this is why it is called the logical table size. This number is utilized by the MicroStrategy SQL Engine to choose which table should be used for the query when two tables are available to get the same data. MicroStrategy chooses the table with the smaller logical table size to optimize the query. Nevertheless, this number can be manipulated by the project Architect. An example of this scenario would be forcing the MicroStrategy SQL Engine to choose a table with a lower level of detail over a summary table.

Warehouse Catalog

Tables are created through the MicroStrategy Warehouse Catalog. This window shows on the left pane the physical tables and views available in the warehouse database and on the right pane which of those tables have been created as MicroStrategy Tables. Once a table is moved from left to right, its definition is saved in the MicroStrategy metadata as an object, a logical table, as shown in the following screenshot:

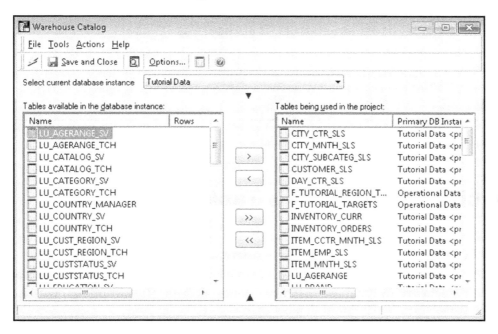

Definition saved in the MicroStrategy metadata as an object

Table structure

Each Table in MicroStrategy has two main views:

- **Logical view**: This view will show which Attributes and Facts are mapped to the table along with information about keys and logical size.
- **Physical view**: This view shows the columns/fields and associated data type from the actual database table, as shown in the next screenshot:

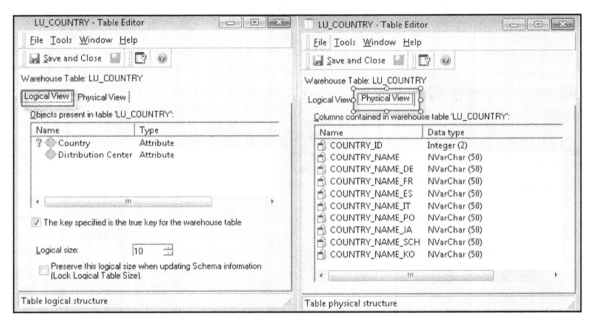

The Logical and Physical view of a table in MicroStrategy

Exercise – Import a few Tables

In this exercise you will use the MicroStrategy Warehouse Catalog to import a few Tables.

1. Open your newly created project **MicroStrategy Essentials**.
2. Access the Warehouse Catalog: Go to menu **Schema | Warehouse Catalog.**
3. **Select current database instance | Tutorial Data**. This dropdown will show the connections to different databases in your environment.

4. Select **LU_COUNTRY**, **LU_REGION** and **LU_CALL_CTR** and move them to the right pane, shown as follows:

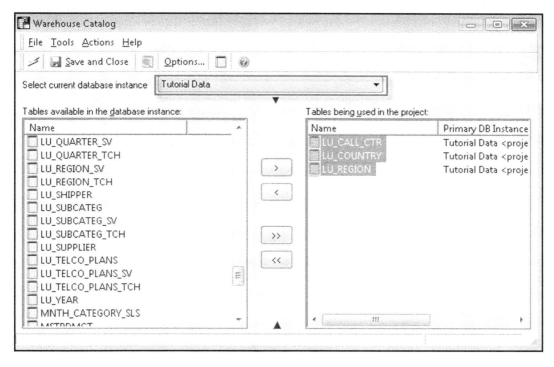

Moving **LU_COUNTRY**, **LU_REGION** and **LU_CALL_CTR** to the right pane

5. **Save** and **Close.**
6. Update the Schema.
7. This finalizes the exercise.

Business raw measures – Facts

MicroStrategy Facts are objects that represent a business measure stored in a database table. The following is a quick reference table for this MicroStrategy Object:

	1) What is it for?	To map business measures to a column or columns in a fact table
	2) What is it made of?	Columns from a MicroStrategy Table (Expressions)
	3) Where can it be used?	Metrics, Object Prompts, Base Formulas

These measures usually have the following characteristics:

- They are numerical
- They can be aggregated (summed up or operated in some way)

The Facts usually map directly to one or more columns in a Fact table. The Fact is defined with a MicroStrategy expression. An expression could be:

- **Base**: an expression which is represented as a single table field
- **Derived**: an expression in which two or more table fields are operated or a function is applied to them

The Fact on its own is meaningless. It needs a context and a rule of aggregation in order to be useful. In the following sections, we will learn about which other MicroStrategy Objects serve this purpose.

Exercise – creating Facts

In this exercise you will learn to create Facts. Take the following steps:

1. Open your newly created **MicroStrategy Essentials** project then import the Table **MNTH_CATEGORY_SLS** and update the Schema (hint: use the Warehouse Catalog). You can refer to the previous table exercise if you get stuck.
2. Go to the **Facts** folder (under **Schema Objects**) and right-click **New | Fact**.

The **Fact Editor** has two windows. The inner one is the **Fact Expression** editor while the outer one is the **Fact Editor**, shown as follows:

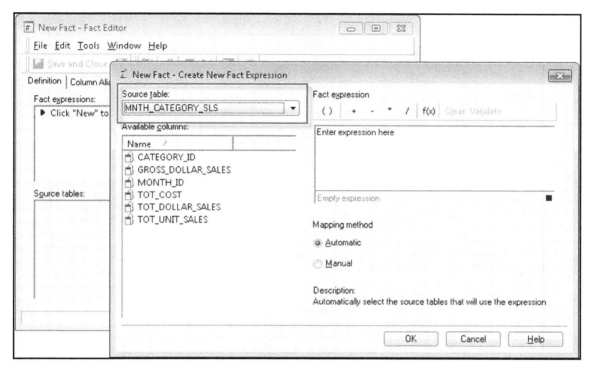

Fact Expression editor ad Fact Editor

3. In the **Expression** editor, make sure the **Source table** dropdown shows the **MNTH_CATEGORY_SLS** table.
4. Double-click on **TOT_DOLLAR_SALES** | **OK**. The automatic mapping method will relate this object to any other table in the Project where this specific expression exists.

5. Review your Fact. Check the expression on the upper pane and the related source table(s) on the lower pane, shown as follows:

Reviewing your Facts

6. **Save and Close** on the **Fact Editor**. Leave the default object name as **Tot Dollar Sales.**

You can update the Schema now or wait until you create or modify multiple Schema Objects.

7. Repeat the above process for the **GROSS_DOLLAR_SALES** Fact.
8. Update Schema. This finalizes the exercise.

Note: MicroStrategy Facts can't be used directly on Reports. It is necessary to create an Application Object on top (Metrics) that will describe the aggregation function and aggregation level for the business measure.

Business context – Attributes

MicroStrategy Attributes are objects which represent a business context, or dimension. The following is a quick reference table for this MicroStrategy Object:

	1) What is it for?	To map business contexts to a column in a look up table. To give context to business measures (facts)
	2) What is it made of?	Columns from a MicroStrategy Table (Attribute Forms)
	3) Where can it be used?	Hierarchies, Templates, Reports, Filters, Metrics, Prompts, Drill Maps

The Attributes will provide the level in which a given Fact is stored in the database and which that Fact can be aggregated to. An Attribute could be mapped to one or more columns in a database table. These tables are commonly referred to as lookup tables or dimension tables. However, it could be mapped to any type of table such as Fact tables.

As opposed to the Facts, the Attributes are not directly built from MicroStrategy but from one or more MicroStrategy **Attribute Forms**. The following diagram helps you to understand how an Attribute is defined in MicroStrategy:

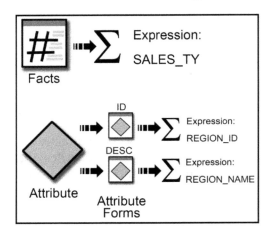

An Attribute form is a characteristic of the same business context. From the previous diagram, we can see that there is an Attribute that has two forms: one is an identification number, and the other is a description. Both columns define the same business context which could be the business region. An Attribute must have at least one form (ID) and could have as many other characteristics as required. For example, the customer Attribute could have the following forms:

- ID
- First name
- Last name
- Suffix
- Prefix
- Nickname

Understanding the Attribute Editor

As opposed to the **Fact Editor** where there are only two nested windows, the **Attribute Editor** has three (listed from the inner to the outer window): Form **Expression Editor**, **Attribute Form Editor** and **Attribute Editor**, shown as follows:

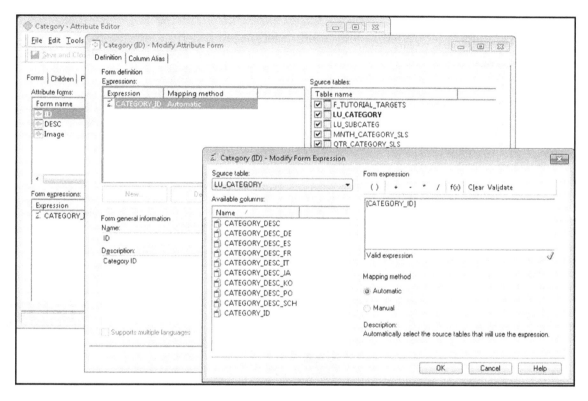

Three windows of the Attribute Editor

The inner most window, the **Form Expression Editor**, is where you define each Attribute form's expression in a similar way as the Fact's expressions are defined. First, select a MicroStrategy Table as the source. The expression for a certain Attribute form could reside in one or more tables in the database. If you want to manually associate the tables, choose the **Manual** mapping method, otherwise the **Automatic** mapping method will relate the Attribute form expression to any other table in the Project where it exists. In the previous image, the **CATEGORY_ID** expression comes from the **LU_CATEGORY** table, and it is automatically mapped to any other table where **CATEGORY_ID** could be found.

Once the form expression is created, you must select a lookup table. The lookup table is a table where MicroStrategy will pull the description for a unique set of business contexts IDs. It is usually called data catalog or dimension table. You can control it in the second-inner window (**Attribute Form Editor**), which is the lookup table, which shows the tables the form is associated with and other form settings such as data type, alias, and default sorting, as shown in the next screenshot:

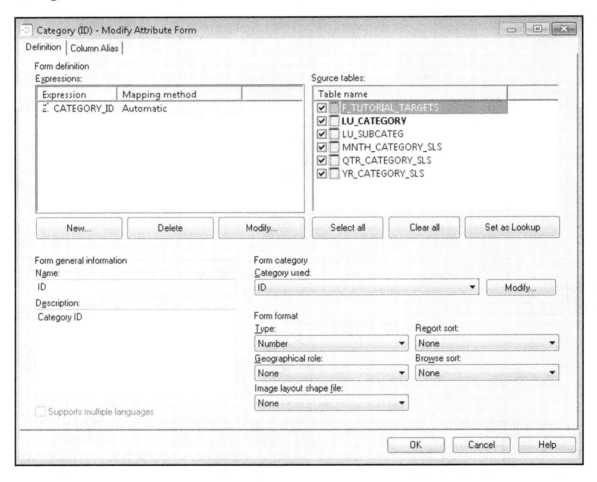

Attribute Form Editor

The next step in the Attribute creation process is to verify the forms created and/or create additional forms. Usually an Attribute has an ID and a DESC (description) form, shown as follows:

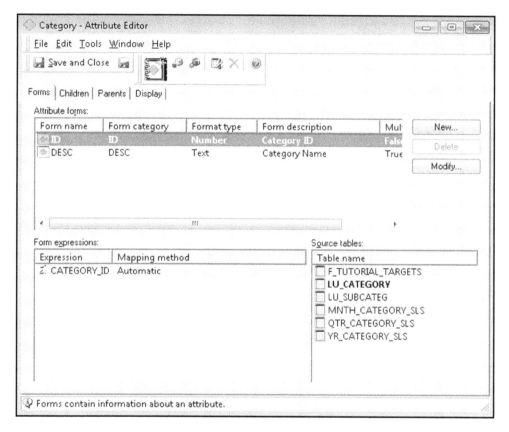

Attribute creation

In the outer most window you will be able to define Attribute Relationships, and see how they relate with other business contexts within the same dimension or Hierarchy. To add a relationship, simply go to the corresponding (children or parents) | **Add** tab, and establish a relationship type and relationship table, as follows:

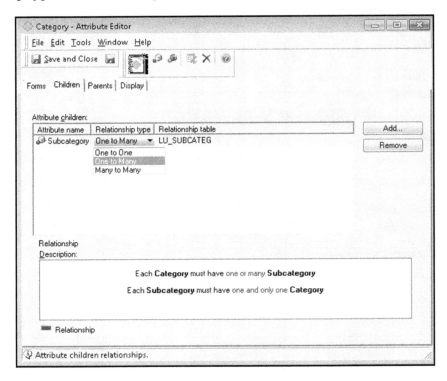

Adding and establishing a relationship type and relationship table

It is important to make sure the Architect understands the data model and how the different Attributes should be related. If you don't see an Attribute or table candidate related to another, it is likely that the data model doesn't support it.

Exercise – creating Attributes

In this exercise, you will learn to create Attributes. Take the following steps:

1. Open your new **MicroStrategy Essentials** project and go to the **Schema Objects** | **Attributes** folder.

2. Right-click **New** | **Attribute**.

3. The **Attribute Editor** will open the three nested windows. In the innermost, the For Expression must be defined. Select the **LU_COUNTRY** table.

4. Double-click on the **COUNTRY_ID** column. Leave **Automatic** mapping | **OK**.

5. You should now be on the second window, the **Form Editor**. Verify that the lookup (in **bold**) table is **LU_COUNTRY**. Which other table is selected? If you had selected the **Manual** method, none of the tables would have been selected and you must manually check which should be used.

6. As shown in the following screenshot, verify that the form category is **ID** and the data type is **Number** | **OK:**

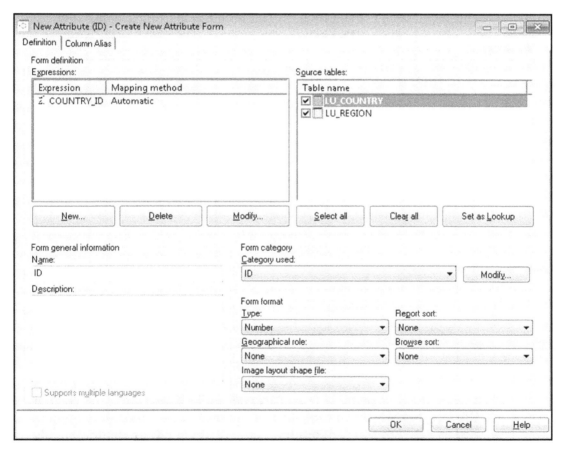

Verifying the form category and data type

7. You should now be on the outermost window. So far only the ID form has been created. You will now add a description for this Attribute. Click on **New** to add a new Attribute form, shown as follows:

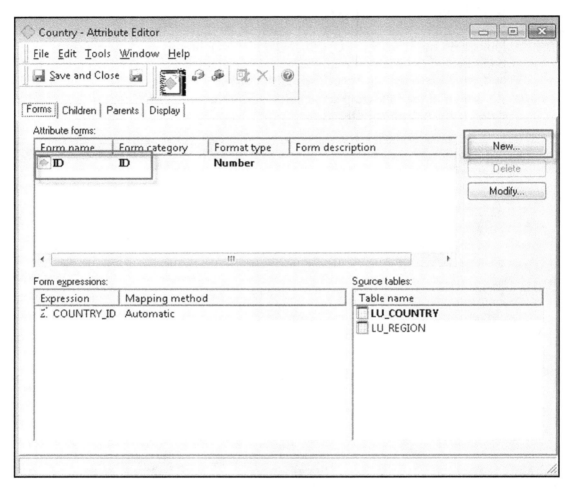

Adding a description for the Attribute

8. Using the same source, the (**LU_COUNTRY**) table, define an expression for **COUNTRY_NAME**. Repeat steps 4 to 6, but this time for the text field that will be used as a description for **Country**. Your **Attribute Editor** window should show both **ID** and **DESC** forms created, shown as follows:

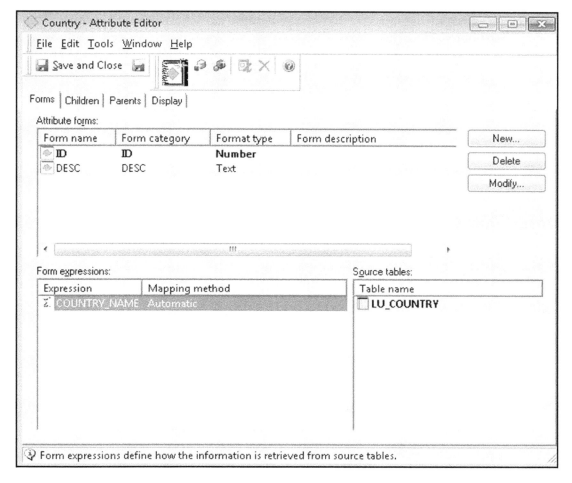

Attribute Editor displaying ID and DESC

9. **Save and Close**. Leave the default object name as **Country** | **Save**.

10. Repeat the process to create a **Region** Attribute with the following information:
    * **Source table / lookup table**: LU_REGION
    * **Attribute forms**: ID (**REGION_ID**) and DESC (**REGION_NAME**)
    * **Parent**: **Country**

11. To assign the region parent go to the **Parents** tab | **Add** | select **Country** Attribute | **OK**. The relationship type and table should look like the following:

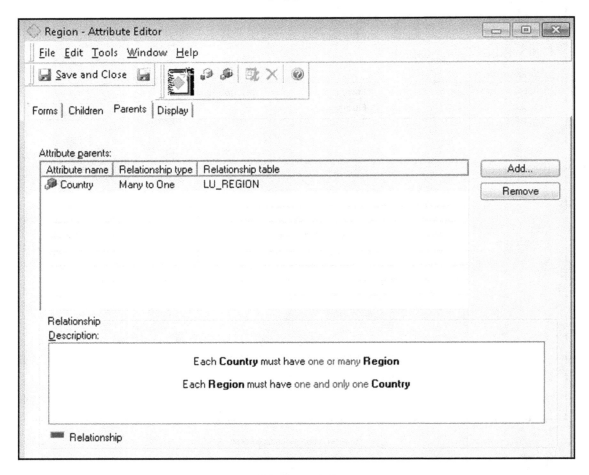

Relationship type and table

12. **Save and Close**. Leave the default object name as **Region** | **Save**.
13. Repeat the process to create a Call Center Attribute with the following information:
    - **Source table / lookup table: LU_CALL_CTR**
    - **Attribute forms**: ID (**CALL_CTR_ID**) and DESC (**CENTER_NAME**)
    - **Parent: Region**

14. **Save and Close**. Leave the default object name as **Call Ctr** | **Save.**
15. Update Schema. This finalizes the exercise.

Grouping business context – Hierarchies

MicroStrategy Hierarchies are Schema Objects made of Attributes, which serve two main purposes:

- Help to visualize and understand the relationships between the Attributes
- Define paths for users to drill (drill maps and drill paths)

The following is a quick reference table for this MicroStrategy Object:

	1) What is it for?	To visualize Attributes, their elements and relationships. To define Drill Maps.
	2) What is it made of?	Attributes
	3) Where can it be used?	Drill Maps, Templates and Metrics (in its dimensionality)

If you navigate to the Data Explorer, you will find the first Hierarchy that is created by default once the first Attribute is saved into the Project—System Hierarchy, as shown in the next screenshot:

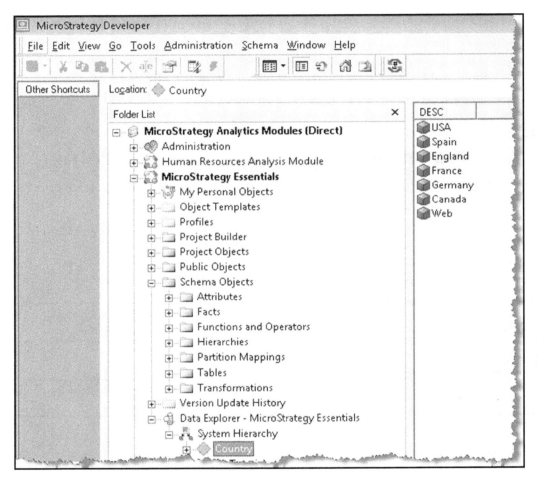

System Hierarchy

The **System Hierarchy** will show all the Attributes in the project with their relationships and their Attribute elements. The Attribute elements are simply the data inside the lookup tables. It is important to note that the Attribute elements are **not Objects** but data instead.

The Architect can define **user Hierarchies** and make them available for final users as drill paths to perform data discovery and further analysis on Reports. In the next exercise, we will learn how to create a user Hierarchy.

Exercise – Creating user Hierarchies

In this exercise you will learn to create Hierarchies.

1. Open your new project **MicroStrategy Essentials** and go to the **Schema Objects** | **Hierarchies** | **Data Explorer** folder.

 Note: you can save a Hierarchy in any other folder. However, to make the Hierarchy available inside Data Explorer it must be saved in the above location.

2. Right-click **New** | **Hierarchy**.
3. On the **Select Objects** window, shown as follows, select **Call Ctr**, **Country** and **Region** | **OK**:

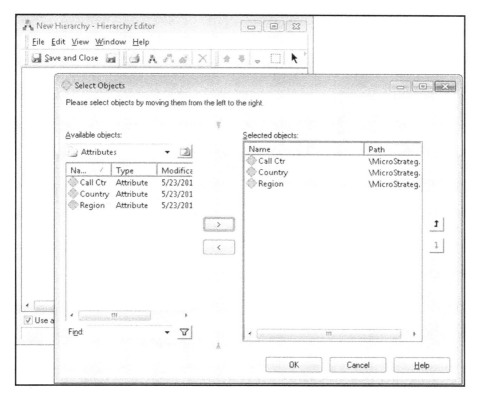

Select Objects window

4. The highest-level Attribute will be selected as **entry point**. In other words, the Attribute with no parents will have a green check mark that indicates a user will be able to drill from it as a starting point. This behavior can be modified by right-clicking the desired Attribute and **Set as entry point**. Note the following screenshot:

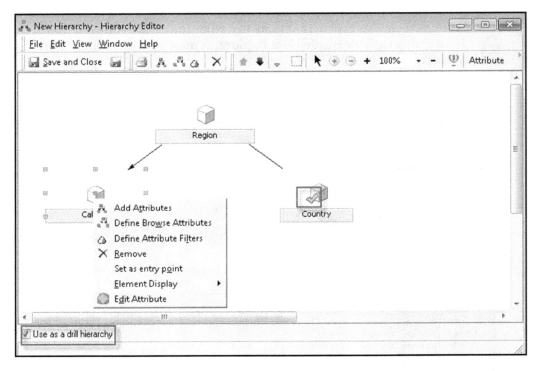

Setting an Attribute as entry point

5. To use this Hierarchy in Reports as a drill path, check **Use as drill Hierarchy | Save and Close**.

6. Name your Hierarchy as **Geography | Save |** update schema.

7. Navigate to the **Data Explorer** (not the folder but the visualization tree instead) and if you don't see your Hierarchy, hit *F5*. Expand your **Geography** Hierarchy to reveal the Attribute relationships and elements, shown as follows:

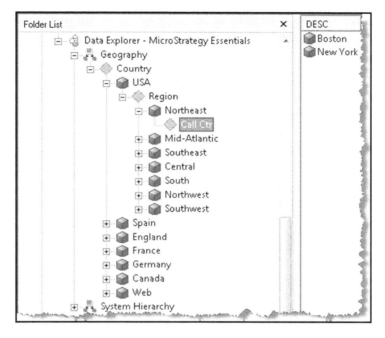

Attribute relationships and elements

8. This finalizes the exercise.

Comparing data across time – Transformations

Transformations are objects that are used inside Metric definitions (we will cover Metrics in the following chapters) to map a time period to another offset time period. The following is a quick reference table for this MicroStrategy Object:

	1) What is it for?	To compare measures across time
	2) What is it made of?	Columns from a MicroStrategy Table (Expression-based/Table-based)
	3) Where can it be used?	Metrics

This object will allow users to perform comparisons between different times, such as this month versus last month, or this year versus last year.

Transformation could be defined using an offset calculation or formula. For example, YEAR −1 to define last year. However, due to the complexity and dynamism of some calendars such as 4-5-4 calendars, it is recommended to use database tables (Transformation tables) to define how a current time Attribute should be mapped.

You can check how table-based Transformations are created by navigating to **MicroStrategy Tutorial** project | **Schema Objects** | **Transformations** and opening any transformation. For example, the **Previous** Transformation, shown as follows:

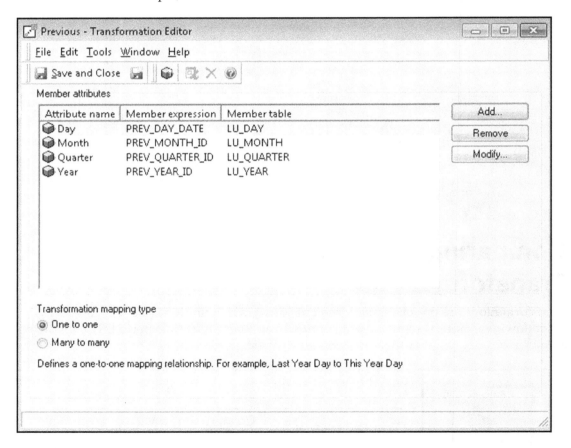

Checking table-based Transformations

You can see this Transformation has four Attribute members, each one with its corresponding transformation expression and where this expression is pulled from. When this Transformation is added to a Metric (such as sales), it will calculate the aggregation not to the actual time but instead using the Transformation expression.

Summary

At the end of this chapter, you should be able to differentiate the three main object types or categories. You should be familiar with the MicroStrategy Developer interface and default Project structure. At this point you should understand and be able to create the following objects:

Configuration Objects:

* Project

Schema Objects:

* Table
* Fact
* Attribute
* Hierarchy
* Transformation

In the next chapter, we will create and manipulate our first Report but not before understanding some of its component objects: Templates, Filters, and Metrics.

Basic Reporting - Building Your First Reports

3

After learning about the MicroStrategy Project foundation and the main types of objects, it is time to build your first Report. To accomplish this, it is necessary to learn a few new concepts and some additional objects. This chapter will introduce you to the Public Objects, also known as Application Objects. Then we will build some basic Public Objects, including a Report, Filters, and Metrics. We will end this chapter with some fundamental Report manipulations.

The following topics will be covered in this chapter:

- Understanding MicroStrategy Public Objects
- Explaining MicroStrategy Reports and how to create one
- Explaining MicroStrategy Templates and how to create one
- Explaining MicroStrategy Filters and how to create one
- Explaining MicroStrategy Metrics and how to create one
- Performing Report manipulations

Your analyzing blocks – Public Objects

The MicroStrategy Public Objects are also known as Application Objects. As the name suggests, these objects are used by the users and analysts (Public), and their main purpose is to create analytic and BI applications. There is usually more than one developer maintaining this type of object. Therefore, unlike the Schema Objects, it is not necessary to perform an update schema after any Public Object creation or change.

Some Public Objects are built upon the foundation that the Schema Objects have created. In other words, some have, as components, other Schema Objects such as Attributes or Facts. There are also other Public objects that are built entirely using other Public Objects or a mix of these and Schema Objects. The following diagram depicts both Schema and Public Objects and which objects are used to build them:

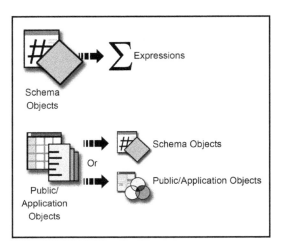

Your main analysis tool – Reports

All Public / Application Objects serve one purpose: to build Reports or Documents (Dashboards) that will allow users to perform analysis. Reports are the primordial analytical assets in any organization.

The following is a quick reference table for this MicroStrategy Object:

	1) What is it for?	To visualize, manipulate, analyze and discover information
	2) What is it made of?	Filters and Templates
	3) Where can it be used?	Documents, Filters and another Reports

MicroStrategy Reports are Application Objects that serve the purpose of allowing final users to visualize, analyze, manipulate, and discover information and trends. Reports are made of two main components: one Template and one or more Filters.

Creating a MicroStrategy Report is a fairly simple task. It just requires combining a Template with a Filter. We will learn in the following sections that the majority of time spent designing a Report is actually time that the developer requires to build the underlying objects such as Filters, Metrics, and Templates.

Understanding the Report Editor

The **Report Editor** has three main sections. Other sections not visible can be accessed via the **View** menu.

Refer to the following screenshot for each section:

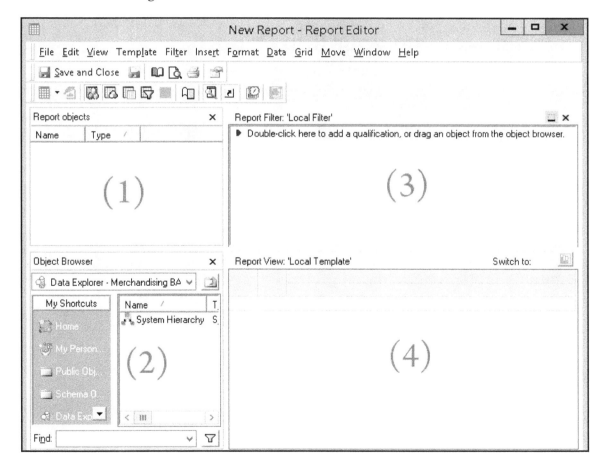

1. The upper-left area is called the **Report objects** window. It lists all objects that are part of the Report definition. If MicroStrategy OLAP Services are licensed, then developers can create Reports in which part of its definition can be hidden in the **Reports Objects** while other objects are shown in the **Report View** (where the **Local Template** is). This is helpful to create different views from the same Report.
2. The lower left section is the **Object Browser**. It provides a tree-like structure navigation similar to Microsoft Explorer and some shortcuts to access the most-used folders. This section will be utilized to find the Report components; either drag or double click them into one of the two above areas.
3. The upper-right section is the **Report Filter** area, where the Filters are added.
4. The lower-right area is the **Report View**, where the Report Template resides.

Exercise – create your first Report

In this exercise, you will learn to create a Report using preexisting objects on the Tutorial Project. Later on, you will learn to create the underlying objects to build a Report from scratch. Take the following steps:

1. In MicroStrategy Developer, log in to the **MicroStrategy Analytics Modules** Project Source.
2. Open the **MicroStrategy Tutorial** Project.
3. Browse to the folder **MicroStrategy Tutorial | Public Objects | Reports.**
4. Create a subfolder named **My Exercises.**

You create a folder the same way you do in the Microsoft Explorer.

5. Once inside the **My Exercises** folder, right-click | **New** | **Report**. A New Grid window will pop up. Leave the default **Blank Report** option | **OK**. The **Report Editor** will open.

6. In the **Object Browser** section (if it is not visible go to **View** menu | **Object Browser**), click on the **Public Objects** shortcut. Alternatively, you can also use the dropdown to navigate to the desired location, then browse to the **Templates**. Select the **Time Analysis** Template and drag and drop it to the Template section.

7. Use the **Object Browser** to locate the following path: **Public Objects** | **Filters** | **Miscellaneous Filters**. Then drag and drop the **TV & Video** Filter into the **Report Filter** section.

8. Click on the Grid view icon located on the **Report Editor** tool bar, shown as follows. The Report will now execute:

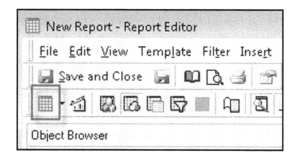

Grid view icon to execute the Report

9. Your newly created Report should look like this one:

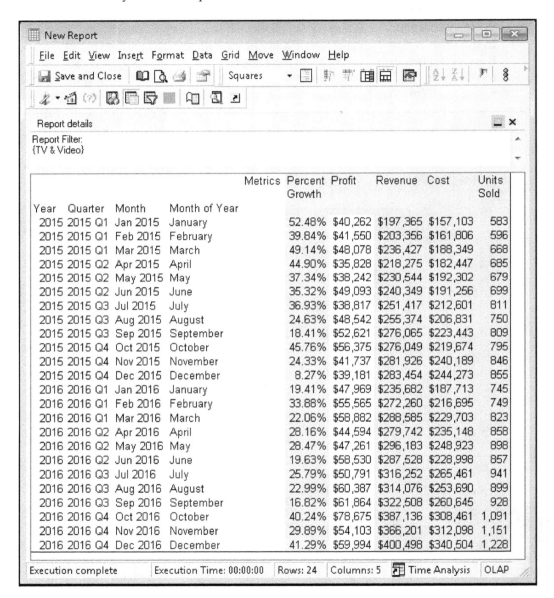

10. Click on the **Save and Close** button; name it **My First Report.**
11. A window will pop up with more options; select **Retain the shortcut to the template**. I will explain the difference in the next section. If a dependency warning window pops up, click **OK**.
12. This finalizes the exercise.

Understanding Local Objects versus External Objects

MicroStrategy is an object-oriented application in which objects can be considered as building blocks. These blocks can be reused to build larger blocks, and so on. Also, they can be used to build not only one but several other larger structures, implying that some objects can be shared and reused. In other words, one MicroStrategy Object can be used in multiple other objects at the same time. However in some scenarios, an object can be created inside another one as a local object. This is also referred to as an embedded object and only exists inside the object in which it was created. Therefore, local or embedded objects are not available for use with any other object definition.

In the previous exercise, we created a Report using an existing Filter and an existing Template. These two objects were originally designed and created as external objects that could be reutilized into another larger object's definition. In the following exercises, we will understand the implications of using external objects or local objects when designing applications.

Exercise – searching for components and dependents

In this exercise, you will use the search window to find an object's components and dependents. Take the following steps:

1. Log in to the **MicroStrategy Analytics Modules** Project Source.
2. Open the **MicroStrategy Tutorial** Project.
3. Navigate to the **My Exercises** folder.

 It is inside the **Reports** folder in **Public Objects**.

4. Locate **My First Report** | right-click | **Search for Components**.

5. You should see the following results (the Filter and Template used on our previous exercise):

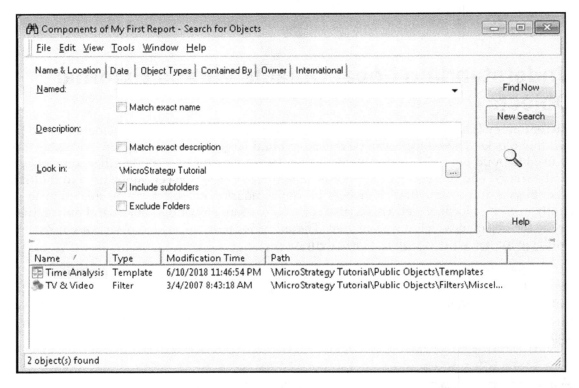

Screen displayed when you click on search for components

6. Navigate to the **Templates** folder.

 It is inside the **Public Objects** folder.

7. Select the **Time Analysis** template | right-click | **Search for Dependents**.
8. You should see the following results (all Objects in which the **Time Analysis** template is used):

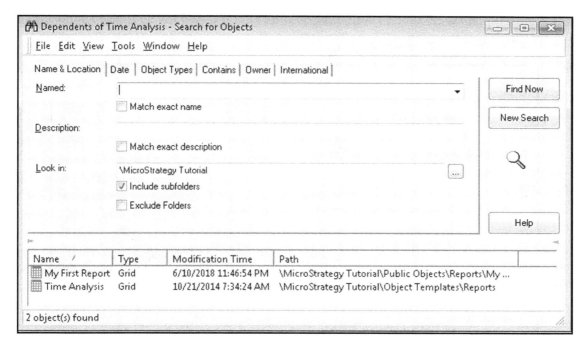

Screen displayed when you click on search for Dependents

9. Go back to the **Templates** folder | double-click the **Time Analysis** template or right-click | **Edit**.
10. The Template editor will open. On the **Object Browser** navigate to the **Schema Objects** | **Attributes** | **Products** folder | double-click **Subcategory**. This action will add the subcategory Attribute to the **Time Analysis** Template.

Note that if you save the Template any object dependent on it will be impacted. This is one of the implications of using **external** objects that are linked or referenced by other ones.

11. **Save and Close**. You will see a window with precisely this warning, detailing which other objects are affected by this change. Click **OK**.

12. Go back to the | **Reports** | **My Exercises** location and double-click **My First Report** to execute it. You should see in your Report the **Subcategory** added to its template with only TV and video results (and limit established in the Filter). This finalizes the exercise. Your results should resemble the following screenshot:

Subcategory	Year	Quarter	Month	Month of Year	Metrics Percent Growth	Profit	Revenue	Cost	Units Sold
TV's	2015	2015 Q1	Jan 2015	January	64.74%	$18,126	$89,495	$71,369	345
TV's	2015	2015 Q1	Feb 2015	February	34.25%	$17,295	$85,326	$68,031	333
TV's	2015	2015 Q1	Mar 2015	March	54.11%	$20,728	$102,867	$82,139	369
TV's	2015	2015 Q2	Apr 2015	April	42.62%	$14,820	$92,222	$77,402	403
TV's	2015	2015 Q2	May 2015	May	38.67%	$15,299	$94,343	$79,044	380
TV's	2015	2015 Q2	Jun 2015	June	26.24%	$19,817	$98,009	$78,192	386
TV's	2015	2015 Q3	Jul 2015	July	25.23%	$16,314	$110,319	$94,005	487
TV's	2015	2015 Q3	Aug 2015	August	10.49%	$18,911	$100,636	$81,725	414
TV's	2015	2015 Q3	Sep 2015	September	6.69%	$21,422	$112,625	$91,203	453
TV's	2015	2015 Q4	Oct 2015	October	23.82%	$22,346	$110,909	$88,563	438
TV's	2015	2015 Q4	Nov 2015	November	43.59%	$18,457	$129,553	$111,097	498
TV's	2015	2015 Q4	Dec 2015	December	3.44%	$16,388	$119,573	$103,185	478
TV's	2016	2016 Q1	Jan 2016	January	15.04%	$20,785	$102,952	$82,167	429
TV's	2016	2016 Q1	Feb 2016	February	15.30%	$19,869	$98,380	$78,511	412
TV's	2016	2016 Q1	Mar 2016	March	28.80%	$26,794	$132,495	$105,701	488
TV's	2016	2016 Q2	Apr 2016	April	31.58%	$19,143	$121,342	$102,199	494
TV's	2016	2016 Q2	May 2016	May	37.22%	$20,322	$129,452	$109,131	502
TV's	2016	2016 Q2	Jun 2016	June	38.91%	$27,506	$136,148	$108,642	515
TV's	2016	2016 Q3	Jul 2016	July	8.96%	$19,358	$120,208	$100,850	516
TV's	2016	2016 Q3	Aug 2016	August	27.16%	$24,066	$127,969	$103,903	483
TV's	2016	2016 Q3	Sep 2016	September	19.51%	$25,843	$134,600	$108,757	510
TV's	2016	2016 Q4	Oct 2016	October	54.19%	$34,484	$171,016	$136,532	626
TV's	2016	2016 Q4	Nov 2016	November	29.55%	$24,455	$167,832	$143,377	669
TV's	2016	2016 Q4	Dec 2016	December	45.98%	$25,136	$174,547	$149,411	714
Video Equipment	2015	2015 Q1	Jan 2015	January	43.62%	$22,135	$107,870	$85,735	238
Video Equipment	2015	2015 Q1	Feb 2015	February	44.19%	$24,254	$118,030	$93,776	263
Video Equipment	2015	2015 Q1	Mar 2015	March	45.52%	$27,350	$133,560	$106,210	299
Video Equipment	2015	2015 Q2	Apr 2015	April	46.61%	$21,009	$126,053	$105,044	282
Video Equipment	2015	2015 Q2	May 2015	May	36.43%	$22,943	$136,201	$113,258	299
Video Equipment	2015	2015 Q2	Jun 2015	June	42.37%	$29,276	$142,340	$113,064	313
Video Equipment	2015	2015 Q3	Jul 2015	July	47.71%	$22,502	$141,098	$118,596	324
Video Equipment	2015	2015 Q3	Aug 2015	August	35.94%	$29,632	$154,738	$125,106	336
Video Equipment	2015	2015 Q3	Sep 2015	September	28.10%	$31,200	$163,440	$132,240	356
Video Equipment	2015	2015 Q4	Oct 2015	October	65.45%	$34,029	$165,140	$131,111	357
Video Equipment	2015	2015 Q4	Nov 2015	November	11.60%	$23,280	$152,373	$129,093	346

Reusing your report designs – Templates

In the previous section, you learned how to create a Report and that its definition is made of one Template and one or more Filters.

The following is a quick reference table for MicroStrategy Templates:

	1) What is it for?	To layout and format the information in the Report
	2) What is it made of?	Attributes, Metrics, Consolidations, Custom Groups, Object Prompts
	3) Where can it be used?	Reports, Object Prompts, Drill Maps

The Template is an Application Object that organizes the information in a certain way (provides a layout) with a specific formatting (colors, fonts, numbers, percentages, and so on) within the Report. Most of the time, Templates are created locally to the Report (embedded), but if the developer wants to reuse a Template, it can be created externally.

The two most common objects used to build Templates are Attributes, which provide the business context, and the Metrics, which provide the aggregation and the business measure. However, we will see in subsequent chapters that other more advanced objects could also be used, such as Prompts and Custom Groups.

> The Template will determine the SELECT/FROM clause in the SQL that MicroStrategy sends to the database, whereas the Attribute IDs determine the GROUP BY.

Limiting your data – Filters

Filters are versatile Application Objects that limit the amount of information a Report shows in its Template.

The following is a quick reference table for this MicroStrategy Object:

	1) What is it for?	To slice and segment the information
	2) What is it made of?	Attributes, Metrics, other Filters, Prompts, Reports and Expressions
	3) Where can it be used?	Reports, Filters, Metrics, Custom Groups, Object Prompts, Hierarchies

There are different types of Filters depending on what are they made of and where they can be used. These are the main types of Filters:

- Filters from Attributes
- Filters from Metrics
- Filters from Reports

The Report Filter will determine the WHERE clause in the SQL that MicroStrategy sends to the database.

Filters from Attributes

To create a Filter that limits the information based on an Attribute, simply drag and drop the Attribute to the Filter editor. There are three subtypes of Filters from Attributes:

- **Qualifying on an Attribute form**: Allows the developer to control the column or field from the Attribute (Attribute form such as **ID** or **DESC**) and the operator (<, >, <>, =, CONTAINS, in list, not in list, and so on) used in the WHERE clause.

- **Qualifying on a Date Attribute**: If the Attribute form is a date data type, MicroStrategy offers dynamic date-filtering options. That is, the ability to limit and offset data depending on the current date. With these options, developers can create Filters such as yesterday, a week ago, last month, last Sunday, the first day of the month, and so on.

- **Qualifying on an Attribute Element**: The developer visually selects which Attribute Element(s) to include or exclude in the WHERE clause. There are only two operators available for this type of qualification: in list and not in list.

Filters from Metrics

To create a Filter that limits the information based on a Metric, drag and drop the Metric to the Filter editor. There are three subtypes of Filters from Metrics:

- **Metric value**: Limits the information based on a value and an operator. Controls the HAVING clause in the SQL.
- **Rank**: Limits the information based on a ranking analytical function, such as top or bottom. It is handled not by SQL but by the Intelligence Server Analytical Engine.
- **Percent**: Limits the information based on a percent and a function such as top or bottom. It is handled not by SQL but by the Intelligence Server Analytical Engine.

Filters from Reports

You can use a report to create a Filter, then use it on another Report. This design will generate an additional SQL pass in which a TEMPORARY table is generated with the inner Report condition. To create a filter based on a report, drag and drop the Filter to the Filter editor.

Exercise – creating some Filters

In this exercise you will learn to create different types of Filters. Take the following steps:

1. Open the **MicroStrategy Tutorial Project** | navigate to **My Exercises** folder.
2. For this exercise, we will create a new Report. Right-click | **New** | **Report**.
3. Add to the Report's local Template the following objects: **Region** and **Call Center** Attributes (location: **Schema Objects/Attributes/Geography**); **Revenue** and **Cost** **Metrics** (location: **Public Objects/Metrics/Sales Metrics**).

4. Execute the Report. You should see the following results:

Region	Call Center	Metrics	Revenue	Cost
Central	Milwaukee		$4,182,139	$3,544,594
	Fargo		$847,227	$720,449
Mid-Atlantic	Washington, DC		$3,135,283	$2,662,083
	Charleston		$1,317,332	$1,117,448
Northeast	Boston		$1,487,936	$1,263,442
	New York		$7,066,478	$5,990,241
Northwest	San Francisco		$1,021,447	$865,116
	Seattle		$739,741	$629,086
South	New Orleans		$3,305,039	$2,800,048
	Memphis		$2,084,241	$1,782,276
Southeast	Atlanta		$1,052,108	$894,145
	Miami		$1,187,843	$1,009,131
Southwest	San Diego		$2,962,719	$2,513,166
	Salt Lake City		$731,413	$619,634
Web	Web		$3,902,762	$3,319,225

Screen displayed after executing the Report

5. Click on the **Design View** to access the **Report Editor**, as shown in the following screenshot:

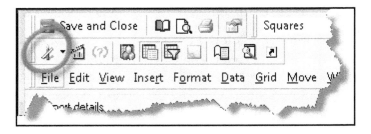

Design View

It is located below the **Save and Close** button. The icon is like a red candle.

6. You will now create a Filter based on an Attribute. In the **Object Browser** locate the **Region** Attribute | drag and drop it to the local Filter section of the Report. Select to qualify on the Region description (**DESC**) and the **Contains** operator. In the Value box write down **North** | and click **OK** as shown in the next screenshot:

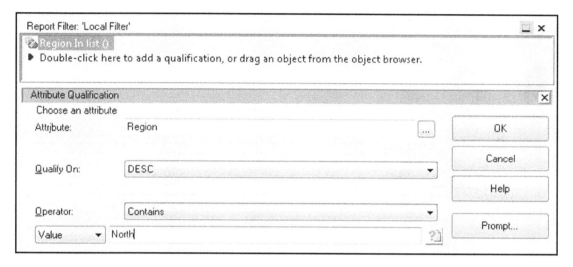

Creating a Filter based on an Attribute

7. Execute the Report. You should see only two regions: **Northeast** and **Northwest** | **Save** and **Close** | name it **Regional Revenue and Cost**.

 Test your knowledge: are the Template and Filters from the above exercise external or local?
Can you reuse them in another Report?
The answers are, they are local objects embedded into the Report definition, and they can't be shared across other objects.

8. Right-click the newly created **Regional Revenue and Cost** Report | **Edit**.
9. Double-click the **Region (DESC) Contains North** local Filter | change to **qualify on Elements** | **Add**. You will notice a list of regions with a red cube. These are the regions' Attribute elements, in other words, the data stored on the region lookup table.
10. Select **Central** and **South** and move them to the right side (you can also double-click them) | click **OK** to close the Attribute element selection | click **OK** to close the Filter Editor.

11. Execute the Report. You should see only two regions: **Central** and **South** | **File** menu | **Save** (or *Ctrl + S*) .

12. Remove the Filter you just created by returning to the **Design view** | right-click the **Report Filter** | **Remove**.

13. Locate the **Revenue** Metric using the **Object Browser** | drag and drop it to the Report Local Filter.

You can also grab it from the Report local Template and drag it up to the Filter section.

14. Qualify the Metric on **Value** | **operator Greater than** | **3000000** as shown in the following screenshot:

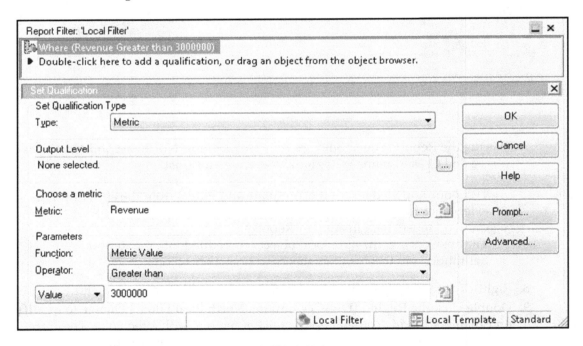

Qualifying the Metric

15. Click **OK** | execute the Report and verify that only call centers with revenues greater than 3 million are shown.

16. Go back to **Design view** | edit the **Local Filter** | change the function from **Value** to **Rank** | operator **Top** | value **3**.
17. Execute the Report. You should see the top three call centers by revenue (New York, Milwaukee, and Web) | **Save** and **Close**. This finalizes the exercise.

Business calculations – Metrics

Metrics are Application Objects that serve to aggregate business measures into a certain business context.

The following is a quick reference table for this MicroStrategy Object:

	1) What is it for?	To aggregate a business measure (Fact) into a business context (Attribute)
	2) What is it made of?	Functions and Operators, Facts, Attributes, other Metrics, Base Formulas, Filters, Transformations, Subtotals
	3) Where can it be used?	Templates, Filters, Object Prompts and other Metrics

The following diagram represents the logical definition of a Metric:

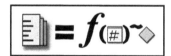

Where a Metric is the result of a function *f* (that can be SUM, COUNT, AVG, and so on) applied to a **Fact** (that can be any raw business measure, like revenue) that is aggregated to a **level** represented by an **Attribute** (that can be any business context or business dimension).

The main difference between Facts and Metrics is that the former is a raw business measure whereas the second is aggregated using a function such as SUM, AVERAGE, and so on, and it is associated to a level or context (an Attribute/hierarchy).

The function can also be applied to an Attribute to generate count-type Metrics.

Describing the types of Metrics

There are three main types of Metrics:

- **Simple Metrics**: These Metrics follow the previous definition. Thus, they are built upon the aggregation of a Fact.
- **Compound Metrics**: These are metrics that result from the operation of two or more Metrics. For example, a percentage change Metric that is defined by dividing the delta of two Metrics, for example, **M2-M1** by one of the numerators: (**M2-M1**)/**M2**.
- **Derived Metrics**: These Metrics can't be created independently or externally like the other two types. Derived Metrics can only be created locally in the Report definition, and the calculations are performed without the use of SQL (by the Intelligence Server Analytical Engine).

Defining the report level

Before starting to build Metrics, it is important to understand the Report level in MicroStrategy. Let's use one of the Reports built in the previous exercises, as shown in the next screenshot:

Region	Call Center	Metrics	Revenue	Cost
Central	Milwaukee		$4,182,139	$3,544,594
	Fargo		$847,227	$720,449
Mid-Atlantic	Washington, DC		$3,135,283	$2,662,083
	Charleston		$1,317,332	$1,117,448
Northeast	Boston		$1,487,936	$1,263,442
	New York		$7,066,478	$5,990,241
Northwest	San Francisco		$1,021,447	$865,116
	Seattle		$739,741	$629,086
South	New Orleans		$3,305,039	$2,800,048
	Memphis		$2,084,241	$1,782,276
Southeast	Atlanta		$1,052,108	$894,145
	Miami		$1,187,843	$1,009,131
Southwest	San Diego		$2,962,719	$2,513,166
	Salt Lake City		$731,413	$619,634
Web	Web		$3,902,762	$3,319,225

Displaying Revenue, Cost Metrics, and Call Center in a Report

The preceding Report shows revenue and cost Metrics and two Attributes—region and call center. When a user reads the Report it could be understood that either the revenue shown is for a call center or for a region. Due to the layout of the information, it is intuitive that the revenue, for example 4,182,139, is for the Milwaukee call center, which happens to be part of the central region. This is what we call a **Report level**.

The Report level can be defined as the **lowest grain** (or business level of aggregation) shown in a Report template. The lowest grain can be from one or more hierarchies or dimensions. For example, if I add the year and month Attributes, the Report will look as follows:

Year	Region	Call Center	Month	Metrics	Revenue	Cost
2016	Central	Milwaukee	Jan 2016		$114,310	$94,314
			Feb 2016		$130,734	$107,482
			Mar 2016		$135,406	$111,183
			Apr 2016		$130,398	$113,318
			May 2016		$143,448	$124,911
			Jun 2016		$132,725	$109,613
			Jul 2016		$140,961	$121,358
			Aug 2016		$138,222	$116,414
			Sep 2016		$156,980	$131,691
			Oct 2016		$163,855	$134,667
			Nov 2016		$168,399	$148,547
			Dec 2016		$186,477	$163,899
		Fargo	Jan 2016		$24,092	$19,947
			Feb 2016		$21,556	$17,804
			Mar 2016		$27,311	$22,505
			Apr 2016		$27,841	$24,384
			May 2016		$30,099	$26,036
			Jun 2016		$21,883	$18,159
			Jul 2016		$37,552	$32,175
			Aug 2016		$24,031	$20,025
			Sep 2016		$27,667	$23,083
			Oct 2016		$27,952	$23,070
			Nov 2016		$25,589	$22,870
			Dec 2016		$31,240	$27,720

Report with the year and month Attributes

Can you identify the Report level? It would be both month and call center. This means that, by default, the Metrics will be calculated at those two levels—the revenue 114,310 is for Milwaukee and January 2016.

 The level in which a Metric calculates or aggregates the information is also referred to as dimensionality.

Understanding the Metric editor and components

The Metric editor features some familiar sections such as the **Object Browser**. It has two tabs, one named **Formula** and one **Subtotals / Aggregation** as shown in the next screenshot:

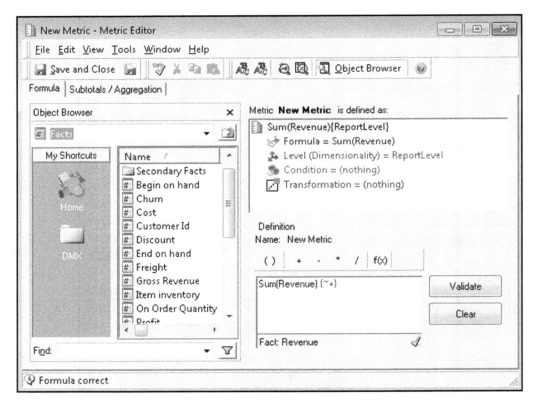

Displaying the two tabs, Formula and Subtotals/Aggregation

In the **Formula** tab, the developer will define the Metric. If the Metric is created using a Fact, it is a simple Metric. The Metric editor will display four components:

- **Formula**: This is the f function and the Fact (it can also be an Attribute but with an f function that could be applied to a string, such as count).
- **Level** (dimensionality): By default the Metric will aggregate at the Report level. This behavior can be modified in this section so that the Metric can be calculated at a higher or different level. This is particularly useful when creating percentage contribution Metrics. To change the dimensionality of a Metric, browse to locate the Attribute(s) into which the Metric will be aggregated.
- **Condition**: To add a Filter to a Metric, use this section. The Filter condition can be added either to the one in the Report definition or treated separately; this is controlled in the condition section of the Metric.
- **Transformation**: In this section, a Transformation is added to a Metric so that it calculates at the time Attribute defined in it.

Exercise – creating some Metrics

In this exercise you will learn to create Metrics. Take the following steps:

1. Open the **MicroStrategy Tutorial** Project | navigate to **My Exercises** folder.
2. Right click | **New** | **Metric.**
3. By default the **Object Browser** will show the **Facts** folder. Double click on the **Revenue** Fact.

 Notice that by default the aggregation is **Sum**; you can change this function by any other available. Browse to this location to check which other functions exist in MicroStrategy: **Schema Objects** | **Functions and Operators.** You can also click on the **f(x)** button on the metric expression window.

4. Leave the other components with the default behavior (**Dimensionality=Report Level, Condition=Nothing, Transformation=Nothing**) | **Save** and **Close** | name it **Sales**.

5. Repeat the above steps to create a new metric, but now go to **Dimensionality** | browse to the **Geography** folder | double-click **Region**. You should see that the Attribute is added to the **Level (Dimensionality)** as follows:

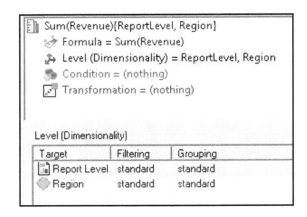

Adding the Attribute to the Level (Dimensionality)

6. **Save and Close** | name it **Regional Sales**.
7. Repeat the process once again to create a third Metric but keep the dimensionality at the Report level and now go to the **Transformation** component | browse the **Transformations** folder and locate **Last Year's** | double-click. You should see that the Transformation is added to the Metric.
8. **Save and Close** | name it **Last Year Sales.**
9. Execute the **Regional Revenue and Cost** Report you created in the previous section.
10. Add the **Sales** and **Regional Sales** Metrics. It should look like this:

Region	Call Center	Metrics	Revenue	Cost	Sales	Regional Sales
Central	Milwaukee		$4,182,139	$3,544,594	4,182,139	5,029,366
	Fargo		$847,227	$720,449	847,227	5,029,366
South	New Orleans		$3,305,039	$2,800,048	3,305,039	5,389,280
	Memphis		$2,084,241	$1,782,276	2,084,241	5,389,280

Adding Sales and Regional Sales Metrics to the Report

Notice that the sales Metric is the same as the preexisting **Revenue** (it is just formatted with the $ symbol) while the regional sales Metric is the aggregation of sales for all call centers in the region.

11. Go to the **Design View** and remove **Call Center, Revenue, Cost** and **Regional Sales.**

You can right-click | **Remove** from Report or drag and drop the undesired object to the **Object Browser.**

12. The Report should have only region and sales. Browse the **Attributes** and locate **Year** within the **Time** folder | add it to the Report's template.

13. Locate the **Last Year Sales** Metric created above | execute the Report. It should look like this:

		Metrics	Last Year Sales
		Sales	
Region	Year		
Central	2015	1,667,004	1,293,634
	2016	2,068,728	1,667,004
South	2015	1,822,819	1,415,767
	2016	2,150,695	1,822,819

Displaying Last Year Sales Metric

Notice that the **Last Year Sales** Metric shows what the revenue was for the prior year. You can remove the Metric to validate that, indeed, the value shown for 2015 corresponds to the 2014 revenue.

		Metrics	Revenue
Region	Year		
	2014		$1,293,634
Central	2015		$1,667,004
	2016		$2,068,728
	2014		$1,415,767
South	2015		$1,822,819
	2016		$2,150,695

Displaying Revenue

14. Close without saving the Report. This finalizes the exercise.

Performing Report manipulations

This section of the book will guide you through the main Report manipulations in a cookbook-exercise style.

 Manipulations (with the exception of drilling) are performed in memory and don't generate a new SQL. Therefore, the Report won't re-execute as a result of performing them.

Manipulation – Autostyle format

Objective/usefulness: To change a Report's color scheme, font types, alignment, and so on. Proceed as follows:

Execute **My First Report** | **Grid** menu | **AutoStyle Selected** | **Agent**. Your Report should turn blue and gray. Try a few different AutoStyles.

Manipulation – Grand total

Objective/usefulness: To provide summation of Metrics in the Report at the highest-possible level. Proceed as follows:

With the Report executed, press *F11* | scroll to the bottom of the Report. You should see a grand total | press *F11* again to remove it.

Manipulation – Subtotal

Objective/usefulness: To provide summation of Metrics in the Report at different aggregation levels. Proceed as follows:

1. Open the **Data** menu | **Subtotals**.

2. Select **Total** | then open the **Display Options** tab, shown as follows:

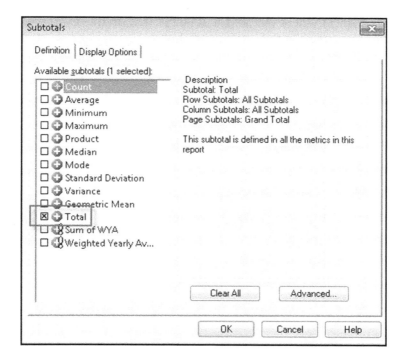

Display Options tab

3. Select the **Top** of each level in the positions by row | **OK**. You should see subtotals across all rows. You can control which subtotals to show through the **Advanced** button within the subtotals window.

4. Press *F11* to keep only the grand total.

Manipulation – Pivoting

Objective/usefulness: To change the order and layout of columns (Metrics and Attributes) in the Report's template.

1. In the Report template, drag and drop the **Month** header to the far left. Notice how the grid's data gets rearranged accordingly.

2. Now we are going to arrange the grid in a cross-tab style | then drag and drop the **Subcategory** header on top of the Metrics header. You can also right-click | **Move** and select where the field will be pivoted. In this example, it would be **To Columns**, as shown in the next screenshot:

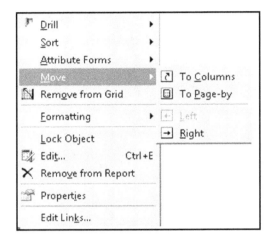

Selecting To Columns option

Manipulation – Page-by

Objective/usefulness: To provide a dropdown that slices the data at certain Attribute level. Proceed as follows:

1. Open the **View** menu | **Page-by**.
2. You should see a section above the Report template labeled **Drop Page Fields Here** | drag and drop the **Year** header into this field (you can also right-click | **Move** | to **Page-by**.
3. Change the dropdown selection of **Year** to see how the Report's data changes too.

Manipulation – Sorting

Objective/usefulness: To order one or multiple columns to a certain logic criteria. Proceed as follows:

1. Right-click on the **Quarter** header | **Sort** | **Descending**.
2. Open the **Data** menu | **Advanced Sorting** | Add the following | **OK**.

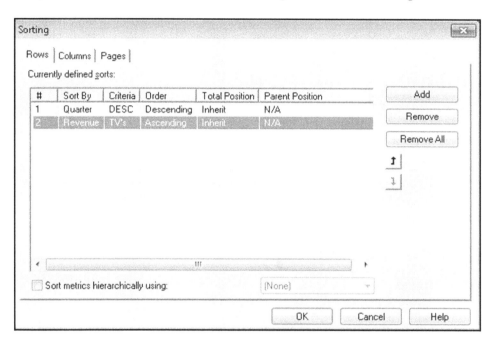

Ordering one or multiple columns to a logic criteria

Manipulation – Exporting

Objective/usefulness: To create a copy of the Report in a third-party format for portability and distribution. Proceed as follows:

Open the **Data** menu | **Export to** | **MS Excel**. Test with other formats such as PDF and text file.

Manipulation – Graph view

Objective/usefulness: To create a visual representation of the Report's data.

1. Open the **View** menu | **Graph View**. Select the default option (vertical bar) | **OK**. You will see a new tool bar that will allow the developer to switch series by row or column, change the graph type, and format it. Try a few other graph types; these are similar to the ones featured in Microsoft Excel.
2. Switch back to the grid view. **View** menu | **Grid View**.

Manipulation – SQL view

Objective/usefulness: To provide a view of the SQL that MicroStrategy sends to the database. The developer can also use it to troubleshot inconsistencies within the Report's results. Proceed as follows:

1. Open the **View** menu | **SQL View**. This is the SQL that MicroStrategy sends to the database.
2. Switch back to the grid view. **View** menu | **Grid View**.

Manipulation – Drilling

Objective/usefulness: To explore higher and lower information levels within the same hierarchy/dimension or across other ones. Proceed as follows:

1. Right click on **Subcategory Video Equipment** | **Drill** | **Down** | **Item.** as shown in the next screenshot:

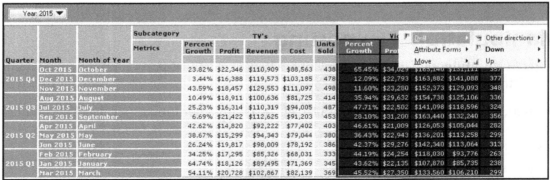

Exploring higher and lower information levels within the same hierarchy/dimension

2. A new Report executes with the item detail for such Subcategory.

3. Pivot the item back to the rows to remove the cross-tab.

Manipulation – Derived Metrics

Objective/usefulness: Create on-the-fly calculations with the existing Report data. Proceed as follows:

1. Close the Report resulting from the preceding drill operation and return to the parent Report.

2. Right click on the **Revenue** header | **Insert** | **Percent to Total** | **Grand Total**, as shown in the next screenshot:

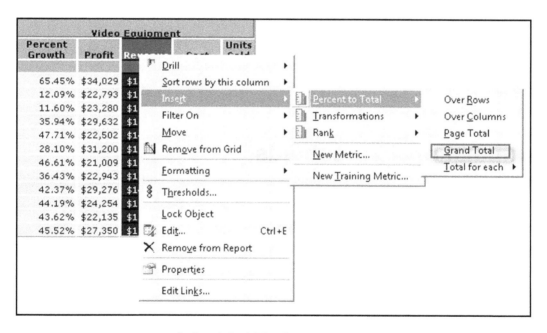

Creating on-the-fly calculations with the existing Report data

A derived Metric is a Metric local to the Report that won't cause a SQL but instead will be calculated in memory by the Intelligence Server.

Manipulation – View Filters

Objective/usefulness: To create on-the-fly Filters with the existing Report data. Proceed as follows:

1. Open the **View** menu | **View Filter**. A section will open above the **Page-by** field.
2. Drag and drop **Month of the Year** to the **View** Filter | select **In list** | Select **Elements** | select **January, February** and **March** elements | **OK** | if **Auto-Apply** changes is not checked, click **Apply**.

This type of Filter is also local to the Report and, similar to the derived Metrics, it won't cause a SQL but instead will be calculated in memory by the Intelligence Server Analytical Engine.

Manipulation – Thresholds

Objective/usefulness: To create and apply conditional formatting following specific criteria. Proceed as follows:

1. Open the **Data** menu | **Thresholds.**

2. In the dropdown select **Revenue | New**. Create the following two conditions:

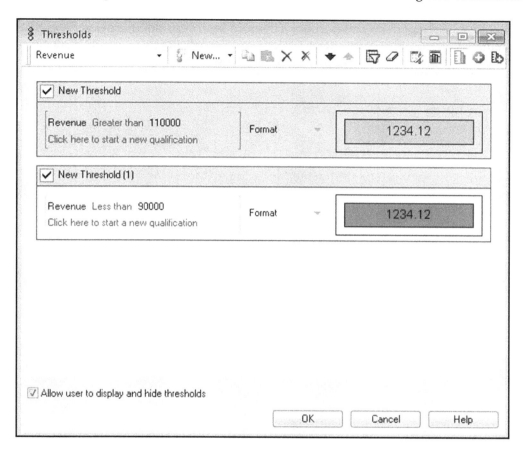

Creating and applying conditional formatting a specific criteria

To format the cells, click on the box with the **1234.12** number. This will open a format editor similar to Excel with the familiar number, alignment, font, border, and background tabs.

Summary

This finalizes the chapter. At this point, you should be able to point the differences between the Schema and the Public/Application Objects in MicroStrategy. You should also be able to create and understand the following Application Objects:

- Report
- Template
- Filter
- Metric

Additionally, you should now understand how to perform some basic Report manipulations such as Page-by, pivoting, sorting, drilling, exporting, and switching to graph mode, among others.

The next chapter will cover some important concepts and objects that will help the developer to enhance the reporting Application, such as custom Groups, Prompts, Drill Maps, and Intelligent Cubes.

4
Advanced Reporting - Interacting with and Improving Your Reports

At this point, you should be familiar with MicroStrategy and its objects, both Schema and Public. In the last chapter, we built some basic reports and manipulations, now it is time to learn about some more advanced objects that will enhance analytics and reporting, adding flexibility and improving performance and scalability.

The following topics will be covered in this chapter:

- What a MicroStrategy Custom Group is and how to create it
- What a MicroStrategy Consolidation is and how to create it
- Understanding the different types of prompts and how to create them
- What a MicroStrategy Drill Map is and how to create it
- What a MicroStrategy Intelligent Cube is, and how to create it

Grouping data together – Custom Groups and Consolidations

When new data is needed on the reporting layer, for example a new Region or a new Product Category, it would need to be fed from the source systems to the database. Then, MicroStrategy can execute a query to report it. However, in some scenarios, due to time constraints or because of a very specific and customized requirement, you might want to group the data in a report to create sets, bands, quartiles, or simply to combine Attribute elements without having to modify the database. We will explore two objects that serve this purpose: Custom Groups and Consolidations.

The following is a quick reference table for a MicroStrategy Custom Group:

	1) What is it for?	To create dynamic sets of data with different filtering criteria
	2) What is it made of?	Custom Group elements (Filters and Bands or N-tiles)
	3) Where can it be used?	Templates, Object Prompts, Drill Maps

A Custom Group is an Application Object that creates dynamic sets of data in such a way that it gives the ability to create several mini-reports inside a Report. This object is based on another familiar one: the Filter. The developer would create one or more Filter qualifications in order to define what is called a Custom Group element. Then it would be possible to show Metrics calculated for that Custom Group element or by individuals that make up the group. Let's see an example. Suppose that you want to show the **Top 5 products** in your company and the **Bottom 5** by Revenue. You would have two groups:

Metrics	Revenue
Top and bottom products	
Top 5 products	$3,833,938
Bottom 5 products	$67,018

Displaying Top 5 products and Bottom 5 products by Revenue

Alternatively, you could also show the items within each group:

	Metrics	Revenue
Top and bottom products		
Top 5 products		$3,833,938
Harman Kardon Digital Surround Sound Receiver		$745,650
Sharp Mobilon TriPad Handheld PC		$715,008
Hewlett Packard OfficeJet Printer		$711,030
ErgoRev Elite Wireless Keyboard		$754,750
Sony DVD/CD/Video Player		$907,500
Bottom 5 products		$67,018
The Prince		$14,878
Lord of the Flies		$12,952
Test Your Baseball IQ		$10,902
The Rules for Cats		$17,237
Test Your History I.Q.		$11,050

Displaying Top 5 products and Bottom 5 products with item names

 Custom Groups are SQL-intensive objects that create several SQL passes. Developers should try to use alternative options, such as two reports in a Dashboard, for the previous example.

Exercise – create a Custom Group

In this exercise, you will learn to create a Custom Group.

1. In MicroStrategy Developer, log in to the **MicroStrategy Analytics Modules** Project Source.
2. Open the **MicroStrategy Tutorial** project.
3. Browse to the **MicroStrategy Tutorial\Public Objects\Reports\My Exercises** folder.
4. Right-click | **New** | **Custom Group.**

5. Using the Object Brower, locate the Revenue Metric (**Public Objects\Metrics\Sales Metrics**) |, and drag and drop it to the right to create a **Custom Group Element**. You will now see a Filter editor-like interface. You create the filter qualification just as you would do on a regular Filter. The only difference is that you need to establish the **Output Level** of the Filter. In previous exercises, when a Filter was created by default, the output level was the Report level, which implied that the Filter was applied to the lowest grain present in the Template. However, in a Custom Group, this level needs to be specified.

6. Create a qualification like this one (set the **Output level** to **Item** Attribute, from the **Product** folder) | **OK**:

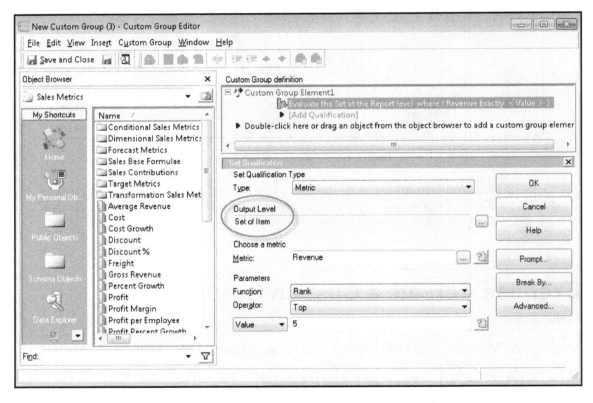

Setting the Output level

7. Right-click on **Custom Group Element1** | **Rename** | **Top 5 products.**

8. Repeat this with a Bottom 5 qualification and name the **Custom Group Element2** as **Bottom 5 products.**

9. **Save and Close** | name it **Top and bottom products.**

10. Create a new Report | Add the **Top and bottom products** Custom Group to the Template | add **Revenue Metric**| Execute the Report. You will see two rows, one for each set, corresponding to the qualifications you created | **Save and close** the Report | name it **Top and bottom products Report.**

11. Now, we will change the display options to show individual items in the group. Edit the **Top and bottom products** Custom Group | Right-click each of the two elements | **Show display options** and select the following:

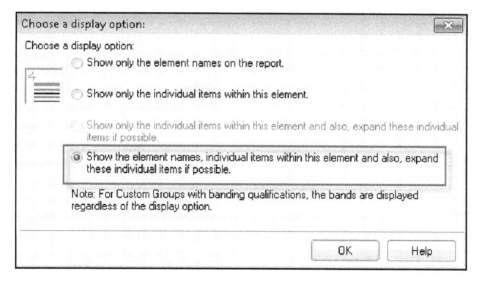

Changing the display options

12. Select **Save and close** | Re-execute the **Top and bottom products** Report. You will now see five individual products on each set.

The previous exercise demonstrates Custom Group elements created from Metrics. This is also called Set Qualification. However, the Filter can also be created using Attributes or other Reports. Additionally, there is an option to create a Group of Bands or N-Tiles (such as Quartiles). To access these options, instead of dragging and dropping the object from the Object Browser into the Custom Group Element, double-click on **Add Qualification**. You will see the following options:

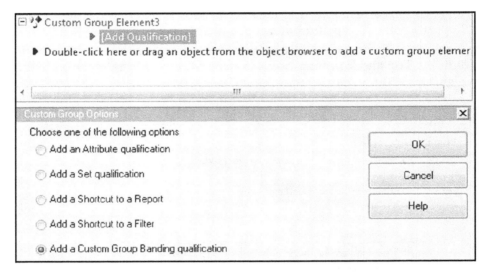

Selecting the option to create a group of bands

A Consolidation is an Application Object that creates static sets of data in such a way that a virtual Attribute can be built.

The following is a quick reference table for a MicroStrategy Consolidation:

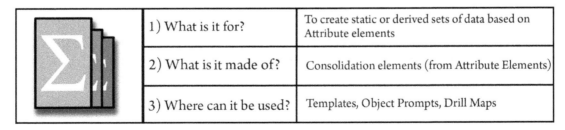

	1) What is it for?	To create static or derived sets of data based on Attribute elements
	2) What is it made of?	Consolidation elements (from Attribute Elements)
	3) Where can it be used?	Templates, Object Prompts, Drill Maps

As opposed to Custom Groups, which are based on qualifications or Filters, Consolidations are built upon Attribute Elements. You will notice that when building a Consolidation Element, the Object Browser shows only the Hierarchies in the Data Explorer and therefore only Attribute Elements can be selected.

Exercise – creating a Consolidation

In this exercise, you will learn to create a Consolidation:

1. Browse to the **MicroStrategy Tutorial\Public Objects\Reports\My Exercises** folder.
2. Right-click | **New** | **Consolidation**.
3. Once the editor is open, click on the area labeled **Click here to add new consolidation element**.
4. Name the First Element **South Region.**
5. In the Object Browser, locate the and double-click **Geography Hierarchy. Double-click on Region** Attribute. You will see the Region's elements.
6. Holding the Control key, select **South, Southeast**, and **Southwest** | Drag and drop them into the expression window. You will see a new expression created: ({Region=South} + {Region=Southeast} + {Region=Southwest}).

You can also use a different arithmetic operator. The expression indicates how all Metrics will behave when aggregated to that new Consolidation element. In the previous scenario, it will add or **consolidate** whichever Metric is on the Template for those Regions.

7. Create another Consolidation Element | Name it **North Central Region** | create the following expression: ({Region=Central} + {Region=Northeast} + {Region=Northwest}).
8. Create another Consolidation Element | Name it **Internet Channel** | create the following expression: {Region=Web}.
9. Create one last Consolidation Element | Name it **Foreign Region** | create the following expression: ({Region=Canada} + {Region=England} + {Region=France} + {Region=Germany}).

Your final Consolidation should look like this:

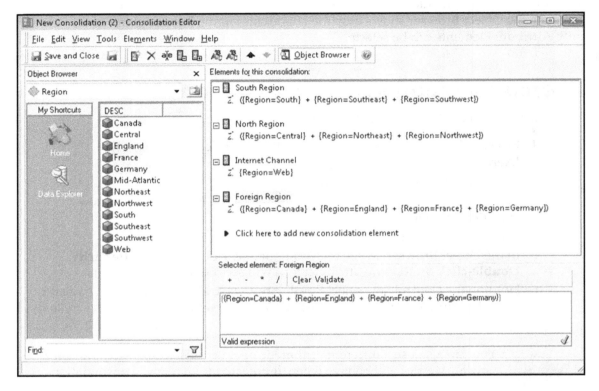

How the final consolidation should look

10. **Save and Close** | Name it **Custom Regions.**
11. Create a new Report | Add a **Custom Regions** and **Revenue** Metric | Execute the Report; it should look like this (note that there is no Revenue for Foreign Regions):

	Metrics	Revenue
Custom Regions		
South Region		$11,323,363
North Region		$15,344,968
Internet Channel		$3,902,762

Custom Regions and Revenue

12. While in the executed Report, browse to `Schema Objects\Attributes\Geography` | Add the **Region** Attribute to the right of the **Custom Regions** Consolidation. You should now see how each Custom Region brakes into the corresponding Region.

MicroStrategy does not validate whether the Consolidation created uses the same Attribute elements on all the Consolidation elements (for example, mixing Regions and Products will make no sense), or if one is missing or repeated (for example, adding Southeast to both the North and South Regions). It is the responsibility of the developer to make sure the Consolidation is created by conforming to the business logic.

Dynamic filtering and report creation – Prompts

Prompts are the most versatile Application objects in MicroStrategy since they provide flexibility to customize the SQL sent to the database, based on a user response to a question that is presented before Report execution.

The following is a quick reference table for this MicroStrategy Object:

	1) What is it for?	To gather information from the user and create dynamic queries for a Report
	2) What is it made of?	Filters, Attributes, Hierarchies Metrics, Templates, Facts, Metrics, Functions, Reports, Custom Groups, Consolidations, Values
	3) Where can it be used?	Reports, Filters, Metrics, Custom Groups, Prompts, Templates, Subtotals

Basically, when a Prompt is inserted in an object, MicroStrategy places a wildcard on the corresponding portion of the SQL. After this when the user responds to the Prompt, that unknown SQL gets replaced accordingly.

Understanding types of Prompts

To better understand Prompts, it is necessary to explain the different types. Their type will determine what objects can be used to build them and how and where to use them.

1. Filter definition prompt:

    -   **What is it for?** To dynamically create a Filter based on the user response
    -   **What is made of?** A Filter definition on a Hierarchy, Attribute, Metric, or by directly picking Attribute elements
    -   **Where can it be used?** Since it is a dynamic Filter, it is possible to use it wherever a regular Filter can be used, such as Reports, other Filters, Custom Groups, and even within another Prompt (Object prompt, see later)

2. Value prompt:

    -   **What is it for?** To input a value using a text box (or a date box or number box); then, this value can be used to complete another object's definition, such a Filter or a Metric
    -   **What is made of?** A text box, a number box, or a date box (free form input)
    -   **Where can it be used?** While creating a Filter or a Metric

3. Level prompt:

    -   **What is it for?** To define the aggregation level (dimensionality) of a Metric
    -   **What is made of?** Attributes and Hierarchies
    -   **Where can it be used?** Within the Metric's dimensionality

4. Object prompt:

    -   **What is it for?** To replace virtually any object in MicroStrategy
    -   **What is made of?** Attributes, Metrics, Templates, Facts, Filters, Reports, Functions and Operators, Custom Groups, and Consolidations
    -   **Where can it be used?** Mostly in Templates, but it can also be used on Filters, Metrics, Custom Groups, Subtotals, and even inside another Object Prompt (nested Prompts)

 It is recommended to use the same type of object when creating an Object Prompt. Its usage will depend on what is inside it. For example, it won't be possible to place an Object Prompt inside a Template if it has Filters inside, because Filters can't be placed on Templates.

Exercise – create some prompted Reports

In this exercise, you will learn to create several types of Prompts:

1. Browse to the **MicroStrategy Tutorial\Public Objects\Reports\My Exercises** folder.
2. Right-click | **New** | **Prompt**. You will see four radio buttons corresponding to each of the four types of Prompts described before.
3. Select **Filter definition prompt** | **Choose from an Attribute element list** | **Next**.

The Filter definition prompt is commonly used in a pair with the Attribute element list option. Try the other three options to see the difference. Basically, these options will let the user build a Filter on the fly, or dynamically create a Filter qualification.

4. Select the **Call Center** Attribute (Under **Geography**) | **Next**.
5. Leave the default option (**List all elements**) | **Next** | Change **Display properties Title** and **Instructions** to anything you want | Set **Minimum number of answers** to 1 | **Maximum number of answers** to 3 | Set **Prompt answer is required.**

If you want to make a prompt optional, leave this last option unchecked.

6. Click **Next** | **Finish** | Save the object as **Choose your Call Center**.
7. Create a new Report with **Call Center** and **Month** Attributes, and the **Revenue** Metric | Add no Filter.
8. In the Report editor, browse to the **My Exercises** folder | Drag and drop the Choose your Call Center Prompt into the Report Filter | Execute the Report. You should see a list of Attribute elements (red cubes) listing all Call Centers in the database. Select one, two, or three Call Centers from the US | Click **Finish.**

You can test the Prompt limits you established: the Prompt is required (click Finish without answering it) and you need a minimum of one and a maximum of three selections.

9. When you execute the Report, you have the option to re-Prompt using the following button:

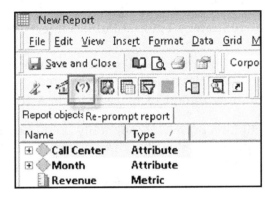

Re-Prompt button

10. Try a few other selections to see how the result varies; also, check the SQL view and verify that the Call Centers selected appear in the WHERE clause | **Save and Close** | Name it **Prompted Report**. You will see the following options:

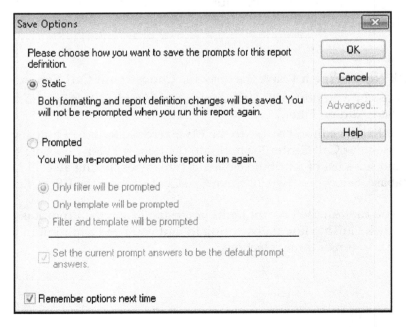

Different selections to see how the result varies

The first option, **Static** , will eliminate any Prompt within the Report definition, whereas the second option, **Prompted**, will keep them in the Filter, Template, or both.

11. Select **Prompted** | **Filter and template will be prompted** | **OK.**

 The first option, **Only filter will be prompted,** makes the template static if there are prompts inside it. The second option, **Only template will be prompted**, makes the filter static if there are prompts inside it. The third option, **Filter and template will be prompted**, will always prompt the user regardless of where the prompts are.

12. Create another Prompt, right-click | **New** | **Prompt.**
13. Select **Object prompt** | **Next** | **Add** | Browse and select **Cost** and **Profit** Metrics (inside the **Sales Metrics** folder) | **OK.**
14. Select **Next** | Change **Display properties Title** and **Instructions** to anything you want | **Finish** | Name it **Choose your Metric.**
15. Edit your **Prompted Report** (right-click | **Edit**) | Drag and drop the **Choose your Metric** Prompt into the Report's Template.

 If the Object Prompt contains an object that usually can't go inside a Template, such as a Filter, this action would not be valid and thus MicroStrategy would not allow dropping it in the Report's Template.

16. Execute the Report | You should see now two Prompts, one for the Filter (**Choose your Call Center**) and one for the Template (**Choose your Metric**).
17. Select **Cost** and/or **Profit** Metrics | Select your Call Centers. Notice how your previous selection is active, since you left the corresponding checkbox marked | Select **Finish** (don't close the Report).
18. We will now create a local Filter with a Value prompt. Go to the **Design view** | Drag and drop the **Year** Attribute into the Filter section | For **Qualify On**, choose from the **ID** drop-down.
19. Leave the operator **Exactly** | In the dropdown below it, select **Simple Prompt** (which is the same as a Value Prompt).
20. Leave **Display properties** as the default | Set **Minimum value** to **2014** and **Maximum value** to **2017** | **Next** | set the **Default value** to **2015** | **Finish** | **OK** | **Save and Close** | Use the same Prompt options as before (Filter and Template).

21. Execute the Prompted Report. There are now three prompts. Answer them, and when you get to the Value Prompt, it should ask for the year | Type **2016** (Notice the default is set to **2015**) | **Finish** | **Save and Close** | **OK** (in the Prompt options).

 MicroStrategy won't validate that the input to a Value Prompt corresponds to the Attribute (in this exercise, Year). It only adds the user response to the WHERE condition. If the user responds with a value that is not valid, the Report will not return any results.

Drilling paths – Drill maps

Drill Maps are Application Objects that provide navigation paths from a Report to levels of aggregation different from what is shown in the Report view or Template.

The following is a quick reference table for this MicroStrategy Object:

	1) What is it for?	To define drill paths or routes to discover information at a different level
	2) What is it made of?	Drill Paths (Attributes, Hierarchies and Templates)
	3) Where can it be used?	Reports, Templates, Projects

When a user executes a Report and right-clicks on any part of the view (a Template with data), three paths are shown by default:

- **Up**: Shows any parent (or grandparent) Attribute from the one where the drill was initiated.
- **Down**: Shows any child (or grandchild) Attribute from the one where the drill was initiated.
- **Other directions**: Also known as **Across**. It will show all user-defined Hierarchies in the Project.

This behavior can be overwritten if a Custom Drill Map is associated with the Report. When a Drill Map is created, the developer decides what Attributes or Hierarchies are shown in each of the three mentioned paths (Up, Down, and Across). In addition, it is also possible to drill to an entirely different Template with diverse Attributes and Metrics.

Exercise – create a Custom Drill Map

In this exercise, you will learn to create a Drill Map and associate it to a Report:

1. Browse to the **MicroStrategy Tutorial\Public Objects\Reports\My Exercises** folder.

2. Create a new Report with the **Call Center** Attribute and **Revenue** Metric | Execute the Report | Right-click on any **Call Center** | **Drill**. Check what the default Drill Map looks like. It should show three paths. Notice how the **Up** path shows Attributes such as **Country**, **Manager**, **Region**, and **Distribution Center**.

3. **Save and Close** | Name it **Call Center Revenue**.

4. Let's think of a scenario where the options available to the users are restricted to some Attributes; perhaps the Metrics in the Report are not available at those levels, or simply to avoid a query that will return a large amount of data. To achieve this, you will need to create a Drill Map. Right-click | **New** | **Drill Map**. The Drill Map editor shows the four Drill Paths: **Up**, **Down**, **Across**, and **Template**.

 You can define in the Drill Map editor which Attributes and/or Hierarchies will become available to each Drill Path.

5. Drag and drop the **Region** Attribute onto the **Up** path | Leave the **Down** path empty | Drag and drop the **Category** Attribute and **Time** Hierarchy onto the **Across** path | Leave the **Template** path empty.

6. Click on the **Up** | **Region** Attribute. Notice that there is a group of Properties available at the right side of the Drill Map editor:

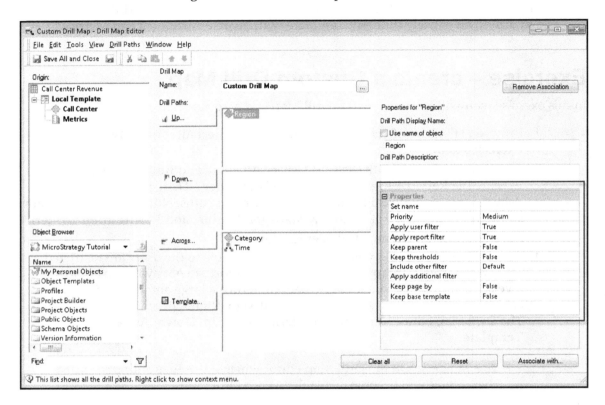

Region Attribute

 These properties will control the behavior of the Drilled Report (often referred as a child Report). You can bring over the Attribute from which you initiated the drill (referred to as the parent Attribute) to the child Report, and bring over the Report Filter, the user selection (user Filter), and so on.

7. Click on the lower-right button, **Associate with...** | Locate the **Call Center Revenue** Report created at the beginning of this exercise | Select it and move it to the right | Make sure **Local Template**, **Call Center**, and **Metrics** are checked | **OK**.

You can specify which objects within the Report's template can initiate a drill action.

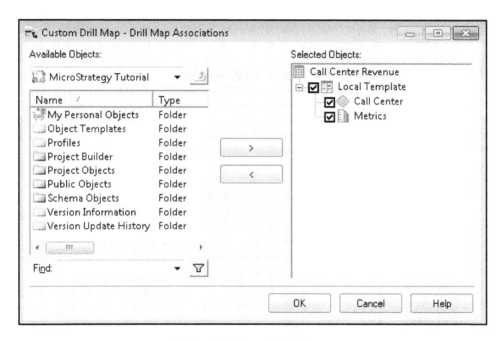

Specifying which options are displayed in the report

8. **Save and Close** | Name it **Custom Drill Map**.

9. Execute your **Call Center Revenue** Report | Right-click on any Call Center | **Drill**. Notice that there are only two drill paths (the Down path has been removed) | Test that the **Up** and **Other directions** paths contain the objects you specified.

10. Drill **Up** to **Region** | Close the child Report | Drill **Other directions** to **Category** | Close the child and parent Reports.

11. We will now create a new Template to create a Drill on the Template path. Create a Template with **Customer** and **Payment Method** Attributes, and **Revenue** and **Unit** sold Metrics | **Save and Close** | Name it **Customer detail**.

12. Edit **Custom Drill Map** | Drag and drop the **Customer detail** Template onto the **Template path** | **Save and Close**.
13. Execute your **Call Center Revenue Report** | Right-click on any **Call Center** | **Drill To template** | **Customer detail**. Verify that the child report shows Customers in the source Call Center with their Revenue and Units Sold.

Publishing data sources – iCubes

Intelligent Cubes, also known as iCubes, are Application objects that allow developers to pre-calculate and publish data sources. These data sources are stored in memory in the Intelligence Server so that result sets for Reports and Documents (Dashboards) can be retrieved immediately, without having to wait for the SQL to be executed against the database.

The following is a quick reference table for this MicroStrategy Object:

	1) What is it for?	To create an in-memory data sources
	2) What is it made of?	Filters and Template, Reports
	3) Where can it be used?	Documents, Reports (Data set)

When a Report uses an iCube as a source of data, as opposed to a relational database, it is referred to as a Data set. A single iCube can source many Data sets. Intelligent Cubes improve performance and user experience by pre-aggregating and pre-calculating the data. In order to be able to create, use, and manage iCubes, it is necessary to license and install MicroStrategy OLAP Services.

The iCube creation process is very similar to Reports: **Right-click | New Intelligent Cube |** Then, add a Template and Filter. There are a few exceptions/differences when compared to Reports:

- It is not possible to add Prompts to an iCube, since the Prompts require on-the-fly changes to the SQL that are sent to the database. Nevertheless, it is possible to add a Prompt to a Data set that points to an iCube. The Prompt will be calculated and resolved by the Analytical Engine with the data available in the iCube, and will produce no SQL changes.
- It is not possible to add Consolidations or Custom Groups to an iCube.
- When an iCube is executed, no data is shown. An iCube that is executing is said to be publishing. This process is what refreshes the data within the iCube. Once the iCube is published, data can be visualized through Data sets using either the iCube or Documents (Dashboards).

To create a Data set from an iCube, simply right-click the iCube | Create Report. To use the Data set, you'll first need to publish the iCube. Then, any changes to the data or structure of the iCube will impact the associated Data set(s) accordingly.

The iCube gets published when it is executed in Developer. However, it should be scheduled to automate the process. To subscribe an iCube to a certain Schedule for automatic refreshing, right-click the iCube | Schedule Delivery to | Refresh Cube | Pick up a Schedule | **OK**.

 You can only create iCube subscriptions on a 3-Tier Project source. Therefore, if you try this in our 2-Tier environment, this option won't be available.

Refer to Chapter 7, *Administration – Maintaining and Monitoring your Project* for details on creating and managing Schedules.

Once an iCube is published/refreshed, it can be managed (deleted, loaded into memory, unloaded, and so on) in Developer.

Refer to Chapter 7, *Administration – Maintaining and Monitoring your Project* for details on monitoring and managing iCubes.

Summary

This chapter went beyond the basics of MicroStrategy with some less common Application Objects that allow developers to create more flexible, scalable, and dynamic solutions. You should be able to create and understand the following objects:

Application Objects

- Custom Group
- Consolidation
- Prompt
- Drill Map
- Intelligent Cube (iCube)

We will learn in the next chapter how to import data from the MicroStrategy Web interface, and how to create and visualize both Enterprise Certified Dashboards and self-service Dashboards.

Dashboarding - Creating Visual Reporting

5

It is time to use all of the skills acquired so far to create visual reporting through Dashboards and Documents. In this chapter, we will be using MicroStrategy Developer in conjunction with its web-based client counterpart, MicroStrategy Web.

The following topics will be covered:

- Understanding how to import data using MicroStrategy Web
- Explaining what a MicroStrategy Document is and how to create one
- Explaining what a MicroStrategy Dashboard is and how to create one

Importing Data

There are times when developers and analysts need a fast and reliable way to leverage a data source to satisfy an immediate reporting need. However, they don't always have access to the enterprise database or data warehouse. It is possible, then, to use MicroStrategy Web to import data into an Intelligent Cube and then use it to build a dashboard or document.

It is necessary to have a 4-Tier environment configured to import data from MicroStrategy Web.

To import data on MicroStrategy Web 10, follow these steps:

1. Click on the **Add External Data** icon that appears once the user logs in to the project:

2. Select the source:

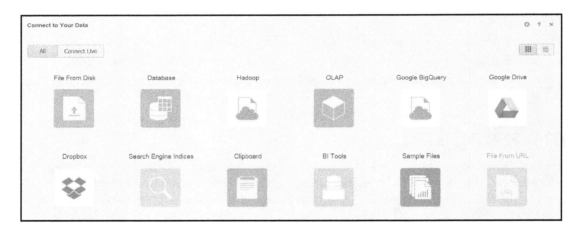

Selecting the source

MicroStrategy connects to a variety of data sources, from files, such as Excel or CSV, to relational databases and nonrelational sources, such as data from a web page. Once the data is imported, MicroStrategy saves it as an Intelligent Cube. The cube can be refreshed and scheduled as a normal cube and used to build documents and dashboards.

3. Prepare the data: The developer decides what to bring and basically converts the data into either Attributes or Metrics.

Exercise – import data

In this exercise, you will import an Excel file that contains data from the MicroStrategy Tutorial database into an Intelligent Cube. Then, this Cube will be used to create a Report:

1. In MicroStrategy Web, log in to the **MicroStrategy Analytics Modules Project Source**.
2. Open the **MicroStrategy Tutorial** Project.
3. On the Home screen, select **Add External Data** | **File From Disk** | **Choose Files** (you can also drag and drop the `TutorialData.xlsx` Excel file). You can find the Excel file in the GitHub Repository (`https://github.com/PacktPublishing/MicroStrategy-Quick-Start-Guide`).
4. Click on **Prepare Data** | Wait until the file gets uploaded.

> By default, MicroStrategy uses the first row in the Excel file as headers for each Attribute and Metric. However, you can add, update, or remove headers and columns during the data preparation phase.

5. Notice that MicroStrategy Web automatically recognizes the columns as either Attributes or Metrics. Nonetheless, you can individually set each to Attribute or Metric by choosing **Convert to**.
6. There is an extra column labeled **Metrics**. Let's get rid of it. Right-click | Select **Do Not Import**.
7. Click on **Finish** | **Save in** | Browse to the **My Exercises** folder | Name it **Imported Cube**, then click on **Save**.
8. Now we are going to test the imported data. After clicking **Save**, there is a window with options for creating either a **Dashboard**, **Document**, or **Report**. Choose **Report**.

9. The Web Report Editor will open. This is similar to Developer. Drag and drop the **Category** and **Call Center** Attributes to the rows. Drag the **Profit** and **Cost** Metrics to the section labeled **Drop Metrics here to add data** | Drag and drop the **Year** Attribute to **PAGE-BY:**

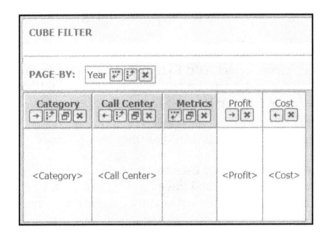

10. Execute the Report by clicking on the top-right icon (a Report with a Thunder), then click on **Report Home** | **Save As..** | **Category Dataset**.

 You can open Developer and locate, in the **My Exercises** folder, your newly created objects. Try to run the **Category Dataset** from Developer.

11. This finalizes the exercise.

Creating enterprise-certified dashboards – Documents

Documents are the ultimate analytics and business intelligence tool. They are Application Objects, which provide final users with the combination of visual representation of key business indicators and interactivity, delivered in a variety of formats (Dynamic HTML, PDF, Excel, and Prints) and media (MicroStrategy Web, MicroStrategy Mobile, and email).

The following is a quick reference table for a MicroStrategy Document:

	1) What is it for?	To create Enterprise certified ("official") Dashboards and interactive data visualizations.
	2) What is it made of?	Reports, Datasets, Intelligent Cubes
	3) Where can it be used?	N/a (It is the largest Public Object)

Documents can be developed using either MicroStrategy Web or MicroStrategy Developer. A Document can be created from one or more Intelligent Cubes or Datasets. Intelligent Cubes provide better performance and deliver a much better user experience since the data is already stored in-memory and retrieved by the Document when it is executed. Conversely, if the Document is based off a Report, when the Document gets executed, the Report (or Reports) needs to be executed against the database.

> A Dataset is a Report used in a Document. It can be created from an Intelligent Cube or result from SQL executed against the Data Warehouse.

The following diagram depicts which objects could be used to create a document:

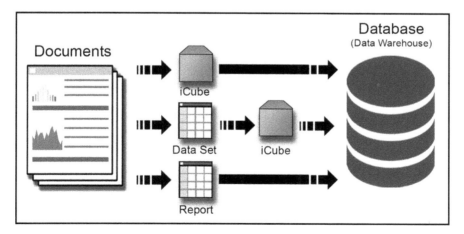

Document structure

The first step towards creating a MicroStrategy Document is to select the Sources (Datasets, iCubes, or Reports). You can always add or remove Data Sources at a later point in time. When a **Blank Document** is created, the editor shows by default the following sections:

- **Page Header**
- **Document Header**
- **Detail Header**
- **Detail**
- **Detail Footer**
- **Document Footer**
- **Page Footer**

These sections are usually only utilized when the document created is printed or delivered in PDF. For dashboard creation, the only section needed is the **Detail Header**, which becomes the **Body** of the document.

In the lower left section of the **Document Editor**, the developer can toggle between **Datasets** and **Property List**, as you can see in the following screenshot:

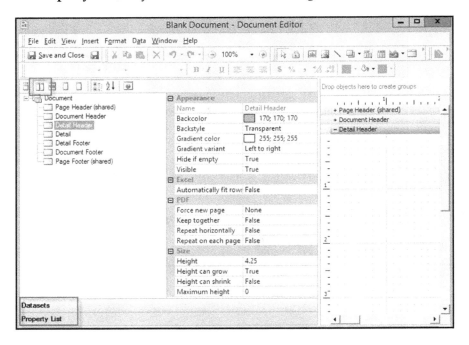

- The **Datasets** view allows the developer to see the Attributes and Metrics available from each source to build visualizations.
- The **Property List** view can be further divided into Document Structure and Control/Objects Properties (click on the icon with the two vertical rectangles).

To remove the unused document sections, go to **Format** I **Document Properties** I **Sections** and uncheck any unwanted sections.

> If the **Detail Header** is kept, this section is automatically converted into the **Body**.

Document controls

Once the data sources have been added to the document (Datasets, iCubes, or Reports), it is time to start designing how the data should be presented and how the user will interact with it. Any item that can be added to the document is called a **control**. These are the most basic types of controls that can be used in a document:

- Text
- Image
- Line
- Shape

There are three other control types that each serve a specialized purpose:

- **Data Controls**: Data can be added to the document as a **Grid**, **Graph**, or **Widget** (Visualization)
- **Filtering Controls**: **Selectors** are used to limit the information of the data controls in an interactive way
- **Organizing Controls**: **Panels** and **Panel Stacks** are used to group controls together and help organize the document layout

In the following exercise, we will learn how to create and use some of these controls.

Exercise – creating a basic document

In this exercise, you will create a document using the imported data from the (TutorialData.xlsx Excel file). The document will feature a grid, a graph, and some selectors to provide the user with interactivity and filtering options:

1. In MicroStrategy Developer, log in to the **MicroStrategy Analytics Modules** Project Source.

2. Open the **MicroStrategy Tutorial** Project and create a new document in the **My Exercises** folder | Select **Blank Document** and click **OK**.

 You can also create documents from MicroStrategy Web in a similar way as you do in Developer. To visualize and interact with the document, it is necessary to open it in MicroStrategy Web as Developer doesn't provide the interface to interact with the document's controls.

3. Browse and locate the **Category Dataset** created in the previous exercise. Once you double click on it, the **Document Editor** will open up. Verify that the dataset is shown on the left pane.

4. Remove all document sections with the exception of **Detail Header**.

 Open the **Format** menu | **Document Properties** | sections.

5. Switch the **Datasets** left panel to **Property List**. Make sure both the **Document** structure and the Control Property window are shown by selecting the second icon on the left pane (two vertical rectangles). Verify that the **Body** is the only section shown in the Document. Click on **Document** in the Document structure tree and change the **Width** to **11**, as shown in the following screenshot:

6. Click on the **Body** in the **Document** structure tree and change the **Height** to **6.5**.

7. Switch back to the **Dataset** pane and drag and drop the **Category Dataset** to the **Body**. Switch to the **Property List** pane, **making sure the newly inserted Grid is selected** | Change the following properties:

   - **Backcolor**: White (255; 255; 255)
   - **Border** (click on **...** to open the window): Remove any border then click **OK**
   - **Left**: 1.9
   - **Top**: 1.125
   - **Height**: 5
   - **Width**: 3.625

The Property window is a contextual pane. It will change depending on which control is selected in the document.

8. Now we will insert some controls. Go to **Insert** | **Text** and with the cursor create a rectangle anywhere in the **Body**. Type **Bookstore Dashboard**. With the text control selected, change the following properties:
    - **Backcolor**: White (255; 255; 255)
    - **Font**: Arial Black, Size 14
    - **Left**: 3.875
    - **Top**: 0.5
    - **Height**: 0.4
    - **Width**: 3

9. Choose **Save and Close** and name it **My first Document**.
10. Now we will test our document. Open MicroStrategy Web and log in to your Project. Browse to the **My Exercises** folder and click on **My first Document**.
11. Let's add another source. Return to Developer and right-click on **Imported Cube** | **Create Report**. Add a **Subcategory** Attribute and **Revenue** Metric to the Template | **Save and Close** | Name it **Subcategory Dataset**.
12. Edit **My first Document** | Go to the **Data** | **Add Dataset** | Locate **Subcategory Dataset**. You should now see the two Datasets on the left pane.

 If the object doesn't show up when you click **Add Dataset**, change the **Object** type dropdown to the corresponding object.

13. Drag and Drop the **Subcategory Dataset** to the right side of the existing Grid | right-click on **Graph** | **View Mode** | **Graph View**.
14. With the **Graph control** selected, change the following properties:
    - **Backcolor**: White (255; 255; 255)
    - **Border** (click on **...** to open the window): Remove any border and click **OK**

- **Left**: 5.875
- **Top**: 1.125
- **Height**: 4.625
- **Width**: 4.625

 If you double a data control such as a grid or a graph, the upper menu bar changes to provide a different set of commands and formatting options.

15. Now we will do some formatting on the graph:
    - Double click on **Subcategory Graph** and go to **Gallery** | **Horizontal Bar** | **Absolute**.
    - Go to **Graph** | **Graph Options** | Go to the **Horizontal Bar Options** section on the left. Click on **All Text Format** | Change **Size** to **10** and **Color** to Black. Then, go to **Display** section | Uncheck **Show Legend** | Go to **Titles** section | **Value Title (Y)** and type **Revenue**. Go to **Series** section and check **Show Data Labels**, then click **OK**:

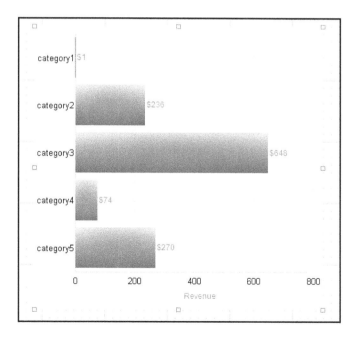

16. Now we will do some formatting on the grid. Double click on the **Category Grid** control and go to the **Grid** menu on the top. Choose **AutoStyle Selected** | **Corporate** | **Save the Document**. Open MicroStrategy Web and run the document again:

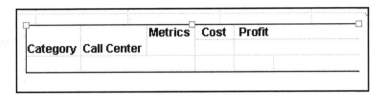

17. You might have noticed that the document is very simple, lacks interactivity, and is far from good-looking. This is because it is necessary to format every control, position and distribute them, and, most importantly, provide the user with a way to interact with the data. Let's make a few more changes.

18. Return to **Developer** | **Edit the Document** | Minimize the Document Editor in such a way that both the **My Exercises** folder and its contents and the Document Editor, are visible at the same time. Drag and drop the **Imported Cube** into the left **Datasets** pane of the document.

If the Document Editor window disappears when you click on the Imported Cube, click on the object without releasing the left mouse button and, while holding it (don't drop it yet), press *Alt + Tab* to switch to the Editor again and drop the Imported Cube within.

19. In the Document editor, go to **Insert** | **Selector** | **Drop-down** and draw a rectangle to the left of the grid.

20. Right-click on the selector | **Properties** | **General tab** | **Name: Month Selector** | **Selector tab** | **Source** dropdown | **Month** | Click on **Manual Targets** on the lower-right corner. Disregard the warning message and click **OK**.

21. With the selector control selected, change the following properties:
    - **Left**: 0.1
    - **Top**: 2
    - **Height**: 0.3
    - **Width**: 1.7
    - **Show title bar**: True
    - **Title**: MONTH

22. Repeat the process to add a selector but now with the **Year** attribute. Make sure that on the **Selector** tab, the **Category Dataset**, **Subcategory Dataset**, and **Month Selector** are selected **targets** | **OK**.

    With the selector control selected, change the following properties:

    - **Left**: 0.1
    - **Top**: 1.46
    - **Height**: 0.3
    - **Width**: 1.7
    - **Show title bar**: True
    - **Title**: YEAR

23. Add a text control and write **TIME SELECTIONS**. With the text control selected, change the following properties:
    - **Backcolor**: 0; 109; 145
    - **Left**: 0.1
    - **Top**: 1.125
    - **Height**: 0.3
    - **Width**: 1.7

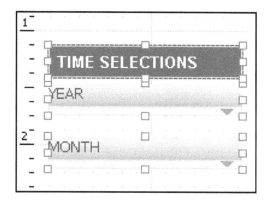

24. **Save** and **Close** the document.

The time-based selectors that we have added **are not present in the Datasets**. If you execute the document and test the selectors, you will notice they won't affect the grid or the graph.

25. Edit both **Category Dataset** and **Subcategory Dataset** and add **Year** and **Month** Attributes I **Save** and **Close** I Execute the Document I Verify that your selectors change the data on both the grid and graph and that the **YEAR** sector also changes the Months accordingly. If this is not happening, make sure the Targets on each selector are set correctly.

As you can see, the grid and graph now show data from all categories. We want to restrict it to **Books** only.

26. Edit your Document in Developer I Right click on the **Grid** I **Edit View Filter** I **New** I **Field** I **Category** I **In list** I **Select Elements** I **Books** I **OK**. Then, **Save** and **Close** the document:

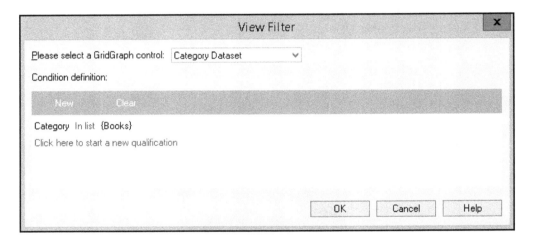

27. Edit your **Subcategory Dataset** I Add **Category** to the Template, then **Save** and **Close** the Report.

This will allow you to create a View Filter on the graph too.

28. Edit your Document | Add a View Filter on the Graph for Books Category too | **Save and Close** the Document | Execute the Document in Web.

Extra credit

29. Add **Region** and **Call Center** Attributes to the two datasets and insert two selectors to the document, one for Region (dropdown) and one for Call Center (check box). Your final dashboard should look like this one:

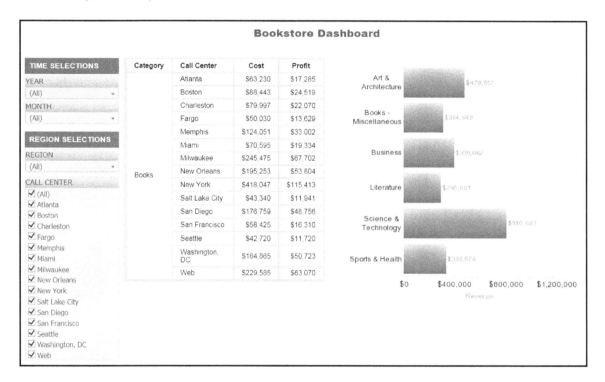

30. This finalizes the exercise.

The documents and dashboards can also be visualized in MicroStrategy Mobile. The same objects might not be used. It is recommended to check whether the document dimensions are appropriate for the device (for examples iPad or iPhone).

For the self-serving enthusiasts – web Dashboards

An enterprise-certified dashboard is a set of reports and visualizations that have been put together typically by developers or IT specialists in conjunction with business partners. The developing cycle usually passes through different phases such as building, testing, user acceptance test (UAT), and production deployment. These types of dashboards and reports are built to be consumed by multiple users company-wide. However, in some scenarios, there might be a requirement to create reporting applications for a smaller set or even an individual in a more agile way. In this situation, a self-service approach might be appropriate to satisfy such a need.

The following is a quick reference table for a MicroStrategy Dashboard:

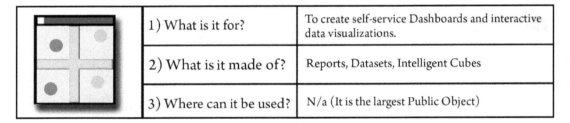	1) What is it for?	To create self-service Dashboards and interactive data visualizations.
	2) What is it made of?	Reports, Datasets, Intelligent Cubes
	3) Where can it be used?	N/a (It is the largest Public Object)

In conjunction with the data-importing capabilities we have covered at the beginning of this chapter, MicroStrategy offers the creation of self-servicing solutions through Application objects called Dashboards (formerly named Visual Insight). It is important to understand the difference between the object called Document, which can generate enterprise-certified dashboards, and the object called Dashboard that is tied with MicroStrategy self-servicing capabilities.

The Dashboard object can only be created and edited using MicroStrategy Web. In Developer, it is only possible to see the object, rename, move, or delete it; Developer doesn't offer editing or creation capabilities for Dashboards.

 If you try to edit a Dashboard object from Developer, it will be converted permanently into a Document so be careful. MicroStrategy alerts about this irreversible change though.

Exercise – creating a dashboard

In this exercise, you will create a self-service dashboard using the imported data from the (TutorialData.xlsx Excel file). Take the following steps:

1. In MicroStrategy Web, log in to the **MicroStrategy Analytics Modules** Project Source.
2. Open the **MicroStrategy Tutorial** Project.
3. Locate the **Imported Cube** and right-click on **Create Dashboard**.

Note that the option to Create a Document in MicroStrategy Web from an iCube it is also available.

4. The first time you create a dashboard, a tutorial splash screen will present the most important sections of the editor, as shown in the following screenshot:

5. Drag a **Region** Attribute, and **Revenue** and **Cost** Metrics to the Visualization area. A Grid visualization will be created, similar to a Grid Report.

6. On the Visualizations bar (right side of the editor) select the sixth icon which corresponds to the Bubble chart.

7. Once the graph is generated, you can control which Metric is associated with *y* or *x* axes by dragging the corresponding object to either the **Vertical** or **Horizontal** box. Similarly, you can control **Color** and **Size** by adding or removing objects from or to those boxes. Drag the **Profit** Metric to the **Size** box | Remove **Revenue** from the **Size** box.

8. Add **Revenue** to the **Color** box. Right-click on **Revenue** in the **Color** box, choose **Thresholds** and then choose the color **Red-Orange-Green**. Click on **OK**.

You can add as many sheets as you want within the same dashboard by clicking the + symbol (similar to Excel).

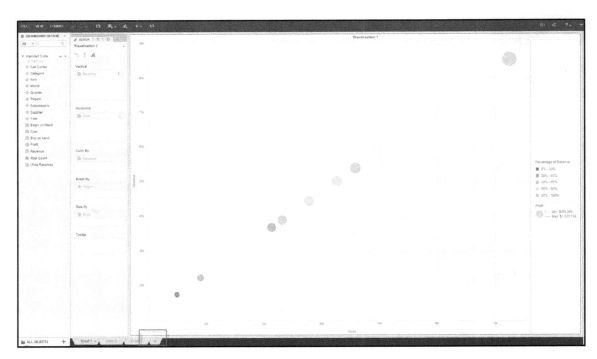

9. Use the disc icon in the top bar to save or choose **File** | **Save** and name it **My first Dashboard** and click **OK**.

10. This finalizes the exercise.

 Similar to documents, dashboards can also be visualized using both MicroStrategy Web and MicroStrategy Mobile.

Summary

This chapter was all about using data to create visual reporting. We started with understanding MicroStrategy data-importing capabilities. Then we covered the following Application Objects:

- Document
- Dashboard

We will switch gears in the next chapter by introducing the main configuration objects that allow administrators to assign user and group access to projects, manage Project privileges, and access control to objects.

Security - Managing Your Users and Their Access

6

So far in MicroStrategy, we have covered a good amount of Schema and Public or Application Objects. It is time now to switch gears and explore objects that will allow administrators to deploy a security layer in MicroStrategy by controlling user privileges and user access to Projects and to specific objects. These objects are part of the MicroStrategy Configuration Objects.

The following topics will be covered:

- MicroStrategy Configuration Objects
- MicroStrategy Users and User Groups and how to create them
- MicroStrategy privileges
- What a MicroStrategy Security Role is and how to create one and assign it
- What a MicroStrategy Security Filter is and how to create one and assign it
- MicroStrategy permissions

Your management blocks – Configuration Objects

MicroStrategy Configuration Objects are objects that share one or more of the following characteristics:

- They don't reside in a specific Project but instead can be shared among all Projects in the metadata
- They are created, maintained, and managed by MicroStrategy Administrators or Platform teams as opposed to architects, developers, or final users

- They allow administrators to establish security, connectivity, data refresh and/or information delivery

As with the Application Objects, it is not necessary to perform an Update Schema after any Configuration Object creation or change.

So far, we have explored only one Configuration Object: the Project. This chapter will focus on security-related Configuration Objects.

MicroStrategy Developer Administration

Within MicroStrategy Developer, there is a section that allows users to manage Configuration Objects. This section is **Administration**, as shown in the following screenshot:

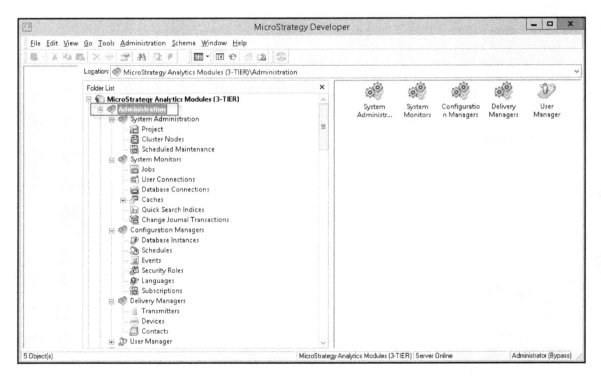

The **Administration** tree is common to all available Projects and further subdivides into the following:

- **System Administration**:
    - **Project**
    - **Cluster Nodes**
    - **Scheduled Maintenance**
- **System Monitors**:
    - **Jobs**
    - **User Connections**
    - **Database Connections**
    - **Caches**
    - **Quick Search Indices**
    - **Change Journal Transactions**
- **Configuration Managers**:
    - **Database Instances**
    - **Schedules**
    - **Events**
    - **Security Roles**
    - **Languages**
    - **Subscriptions**
- **Delivery Managers**:
    - **Transmitters**
    - **Devices**
    - **Contacts**
- **User Manager**

These sections are only visible on a 3-Tier Project Source.

In this chapter, we will work mainly with the **User Manager** section while the next chapter will cover some **System Monitors** and **Configuration Managers**.

MicroStrategy security levels

There are three levels of security deployed within MicroStrategy. These levels are depicted in the following diagram:

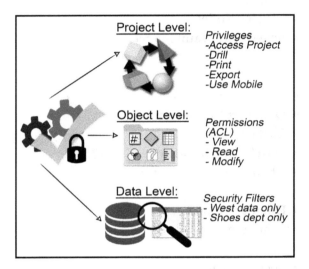

Project-level security

This level applies to an entire Project. The objects used to enforce Project-level security are:

- Users
- User Groups
- Security Roles

These three objects could grant or constrain functionality within a Project.

It is key to understand the difference between a MicroStrategy **privilege** and a **permission**. The **privilege** is always tied to functionality. That is, what a user can or can't do on a given Project and with a given client application. Examples of privileges are report manipulations such as sort, drill, print, and export; use of object editors for developing purposes such as the use of Document or Intelligent Cube editors; and use of certain client applications such as Integrity Manager, Object Manager, and MicroStrategy Mobile, to mention a few. The **permissions**, on the other hand, are tied to access to objects and folders within a Project.

Privileges within MicroStrategy can be assigned by creating Users, Groups, and Security Roles. The privileges are separated by application and then functionality, as shown in the following screenshot:

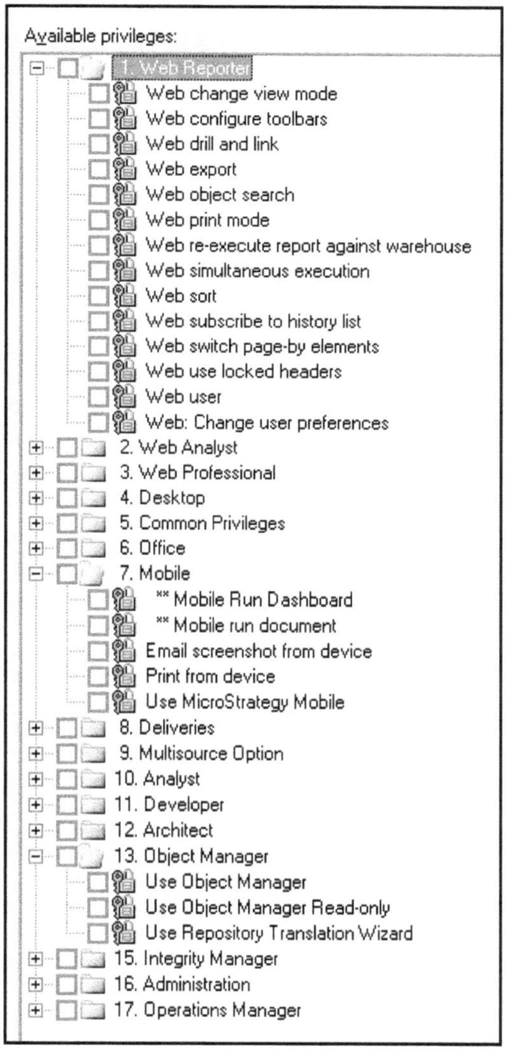

For MicroStrategy version 10.x, the complete list of privileges and their descriptions can be found here:

```
https://www2.microstrategy.com/producthelp/10.5/SupplementalAdmin/WebHelp/Lang_
1033/Content/AdminSupplemental/List_of_all_privileges.htm
```

You can Google *MicroStrategy list of all privileges version x* to find such a list for a specific MicroStrategy version.

Profiles for accessing Projects – Users and Groups

Users are MicroStrategy Configuration Objects utilized to create profiles to access MicroStrategy platform tools, capabilities, functionalities, and Projects. Because Users reside within the MicroStrategy Metadata, it allows you to employ the same object across all different tools and servers to authenticate and dictate what and how MicroStrategy should be used. As a Configuration Object, a User is not created within a specific Project, but instead is to be shared among available projects. To create and manage Users, you can utilize MicroStrategy Developer's **Administrator** tree | **User Manager**.

The following is a quick reference table for MicroStrategy Users:

	1) What is it for?	To represent user profiles
	2) What is it made of?	Authentication type, privileges, Security Roles, Security Filters
	3) Where can it be used?	User Groups

Exercise – creating your first User

In this exercise, you will create a MicroStrategy User providing access to a MicroStrategy Tutorial Project:

> 1. In MicroStrategy Developer, log in to the **MicroStrategy Analytics Modules** Project Source.

2. Open **Administration** | **User Manager**. You will see that, by default, there are two objects already created for the Tutorial Metadata: **Everyone** and **MicroStrategy Groups**. These are User Groups and within there are Users.

The **Everyone** Group is a MicroStrategy out-of-the-box User Group to which every User is member. This group can be used to assign privileges to every single user.

3. Double-click the **Everyone** Group | Right-click and choose | **New User** | The User Editor will open.

4. In the **User Definition** section select **General** | **login smith** | **Full name Donald smith**.

5. Assign any password you like.

As Administrator, you can reset users' forgotten passwords and select the option **User must change password at next logon**.

6. Leave the rest of the settings as default. Verify though that there are other available options that allow administrators to control how the passwords are set and their expiration. Click **OK**.

7. The user has been created at this point but no privilege has been given or Project access so far. Log out of the Project Source | Right-click and choose **Disconnect from Project Source**.

8. Log back in but as the newly created User **smith**. You will see that there are no Projects displayed on Developer. A message is shown instead: **No Projects were returned by this project source**.

9. Log out from the **smith** session | Log in as **administrator** | Open the **Administration** tree | **User Manager** | **Everyone** | locate the **smith** User | Right-click and choose **Edit**.

10. Go to the **User Definition** section in the left panel and click on **Project Access**. It is recommended to maximize the window to better visualize the Projects and Privileges assigned. In this section, administrators grant or deny access to Projects and which privileges are associated to each User (similarly, privileges for Groups are set in this section too).

11. Under the **Analyst** set of privileges, check **Use Developer**. Note how all three checkmarks are granted for the three Projects at the same time, as shown in the following screenshot:

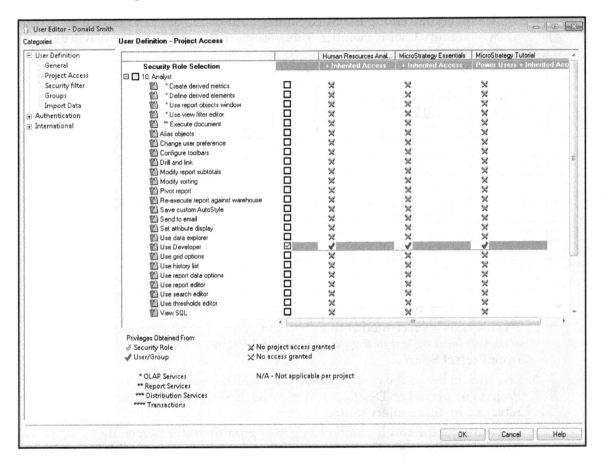

12. Click **OK** | Log out from **administrator** | Log back in as **smith**. You should be able to see the **MicroStrategy Tutorial** Project. The other two Projects are shown as well.

If different Projects require a different set of privileges and access level, a Security Role needs to be created and applied accordingly. We will cover this later on.

13. This finalizes the exercise.

While it is easy to create a User and assign privileges, it could be a daunting task to assign such access for hundreds or even thousands of users. If several users share similar access and privileges, the administrator can create User Groups and then add Users as members to them.

The following is a quick reference table for MicroStrategy User Groups:

	1) What is it for?	To create sets of users with similar profiles
	2) What is it made of?	Authentication type, privileges, Security Roles, Security Filters, Users, User Groups (Subgroups)
	3) Where can it be used?	User Groups

A User Group is a Configuration Object with a set of privileges shared with User members (such as user roles). The User's privileges will then merge with whatever other set of privileges are assigned to its parent Group. This is called inherited access.

Exercise – creating a User Group

In this exercise you will create a User Group, assign some privileges to it, and add the User **smith** as a member. Take the following steps:

1. In MicroStrategy Developer, log in as the newly created User **smith** to the **MicroStrategy Analytics Modules** Project Source.
2. Open **MicroStrategy Tutorial Project** | Navigate to the **My Exercises** folder | Try to edit **My First Report**. You will note that you can't edit it. This is because no other privilege has been granted to **smith**.
3. Log out from the **smith** session | Log in as **administrator** | Open the **Administration** tree | **User Manager** | Right-click | **New** | **Group** | Name it **Developing Team**.
4. Go to the **Group Definition** section on the left panel | **Project Access**. We will assign a set of Privileges to this Group. Check all **Analyst** privileges (you can check the **Analyst** privileges set and all underlying Privileges will be selected) and all **Developer** privileges.

5. Go to the **Members** section on the left panel I **Add** I in the **Available members** dropdown select the **Everyone** I **donald** I Make sure that the **Show users check mark** is selected I Click on the Find funnel to show the results I User **smith** should be returned I Move it to the right panel I **OK** I **OK** to close the Group editor:

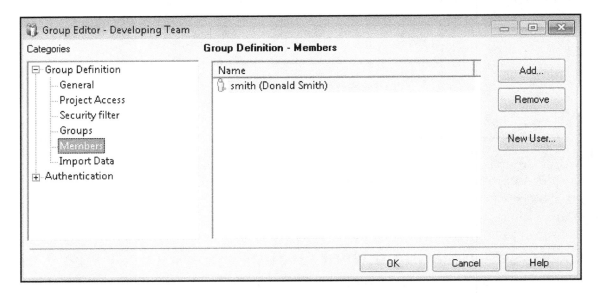

6. Under **User Manager** I **Developing Team** I Make sure that the **smith** user shows up under that Group.

If you edit the user **smith** I **User Definition** I **Project Access**, you will note that the **Analyst** and **Developer** privileges set is checked now. Also under **User Definition** I **Groups**, you will see that **Developing Team** is checked. Here administrators can also manage group memberships.

7. Log out from the **administrator** session I Log in as **smith** I Navigate to the **My Exercises** folder within **MicroStrategy Tutorial** I locate **My First Report** and verify that you can edit the Report now.

8. This finalizes the exercise.

Grouping privileges together – Security Roles

When privileges are assigned to a User or a Group, they are applied to any Project they have access to. Unless there is a role that requires always the same level of access regardless of the Project, such as the Administrator or a Power Architect, this security design is not recommended. A Security Role is necessary to provide different levels of access and privilege sets to different Projects.

The following is a quick reference table for a MicroStrategy Security Role:

	1) What is it for?	To create sets of privileges
	2) What is it made of?	Privileges
	3) Where can it be used?	Users and User Groups

A Security Role is a Configuration Object with a set of privileges that can be associated to Users and Groups for a specific Project.

The main difference with User and Group privileges is that Security Roles apply the privileges on a project-by-project basis. This allows administrators to fine tune the level of access and functionality for Users and Groups, depending on the Project and not on the User Role. With Security Role, a user such as **smith** could have almost administrative privileges in one Project while only Report execution in another and even no access to a third one.

Exercise – creating and assign a Security Role

In this exercise, you will create two Security Roles and assign them to the User **smith** for specific Project access. Take the following steps:

1. In MicroStrategy Developer, log in as **administrator** to the **MicroStrategy Analytics Modules** Project Source.
2. Open the **Administration** Tree | **Configuration Managers** | **Security Roles**. By default you will see some roles created for the Tutorial Projects.

3. Right-click | **New** | **Security Role** | Name it **Basic Access** | **OK**.

Note that no privilege has been given for this Security Role.

4. Right-click | **New** | **Security Role** | Name it **Admin Access** | Go to the **Privileges** tab | Check **Administration** privileges set | There will be a warning message stating that there is a privilege that will bypass any restriction giving the users full control over all objects. Click **OK** | **OK** again to close the Security Role editor.

Now we will edit the **Everyone** Group. This is an out-of-the-box User Group of which every other Group and User is a member. It is a good practice to remove any privilege and/or Security Role from this Group since it will inherit them to every User in the Project.

5. Edit the **Everyone** Group | Go to **Group Definition** | **Project Access** | click under the **MicroStrategy Tutorial Project (Security Role Selection**, where **Normal Users** is shown). A drop down menu will appear with available Security Roles | Select the first option, which basically blanks the Group. Repeat this process for the other two Projects (**Human Resources Analysis Modules** and **MicroStrategy Essentials**) | **OK**.

6. Edit the User **smith** | Go to **User Definition** | **Project Access** | Assign to **MicroStrategy Tutorial** Project the **Admin Access** Security Role | Assign to **MicroStrategy Essentials** Project the **Basic Access** Security Role | Leave **Human Resources Analysis Modules** with the default Blank | **OK**.

The User **smith** will still have access to **MicroStrategy Essentials** since it inherits the privileges from the parent Group, while the access to **Human Resources Analysis Modules** is null.

You can check the privileges for the User **smith** and verify that all of them are grayed out under **Human Resources Analysis Modules**, as shown in the following screenshot:

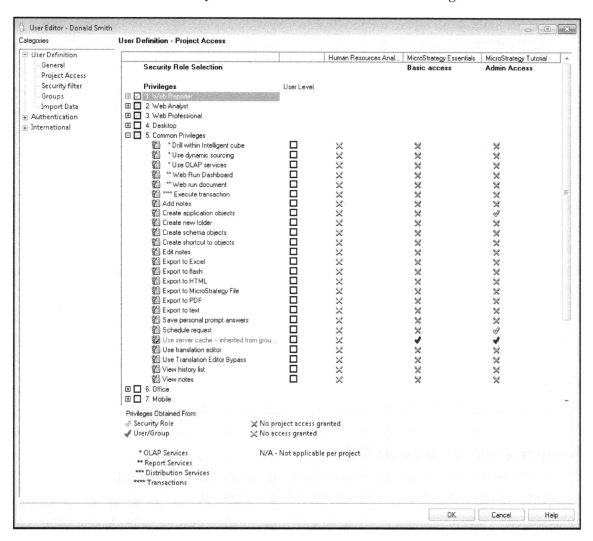

7. Log in as the User **smith** | Verify that, **Human Resources Analysis Modules Project** is not visible | Verify that in **MicroStrategy Tutorial**, you can edit, rename, and create new objects, whereas in **MicroStrategy Essentials** the access is limited (no renaming and no new object creation).

8. This finalizes the exercise.

The following diagram describes how privileges affect Users, User Groups, and Projects:

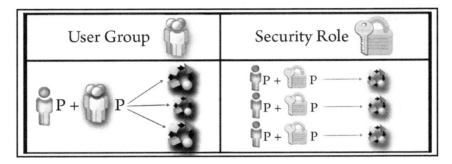

When a User is member of a **User Group**, it will inherit the Group's privileges (union of privileges) and the resulting set will apply to all Projects. On the other hand, when a User (or User Group too) has a Security Role associated, the resulting set is applicable to a specific Project.

 Special scenario: When no Security Role is applied and there is no role inherited from parent Groups such as Everyone, the role is blanked and the access to the Project in turn is completely denied.

Object-level security

This level applies to an object or group of objects (including folders and subfolders) within a Project. The **permissions** are used to enforce Object level.

As opposed to **privileges**, which are related to functionality, **permissions** are related to Object access. Permissions dictate the **Access Control List** (also known as **ACL**) of every object within the Project.

Object-level security is set by right-clicking on the desired object or folder | **Properties** | **Security**, as shown in the following screenshot:

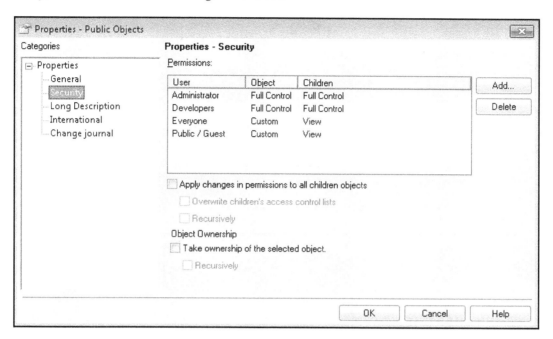

In this window, administrators can establish which Users and User Groups have access to a specific object and/or children (underlying objects and subfolders). In addition, the User in session can take ownership of the object and/or children.

Permissions

There are seven types of permissions in MicroStrategy:

- **Browse**: Allows users to **see** the Object:
    - Additional permissions required:
        - None

- **Read**: Allows users to **open** the Object editor (but not to make any change or save it):
    - Additional permissions required:
        - Browse

- **Write**: Allows users to **change** and **save** the Object:
  - Additional permissions required:
    - Browse
    - Read

- **Delete**: Allows users to **delete** the Object:
  - Additional permissions required:
    - Browse
    - Write

- **Control**: Allows users to **change** the **ACL** of the Object:
  - Additional permissions required:
    - Browse
    - Read

- **Use**: Allows users to **use** the Object as part of the definition of another one:
  - Additional permissions required:
    - Browse
    - Read

- **Execute**: Allows users to **execute** a Report or an Intelligent Cube. If this permission is denied to a Report component such as a Metric or Attribute, the parent Report will not execute:
  - Additional permissions required:
    - Browse

When a user tries to perform an operation that is not allowed by the ACL, it will get an error such as the following:

Report: My First Report (Cont)
Status: Initialization Failed

Error: You do not have Execute access to the Report Definition object 'My First Report (Cont)'.

Starting Time: 00:13:48

Or the user will get something similar to this one:

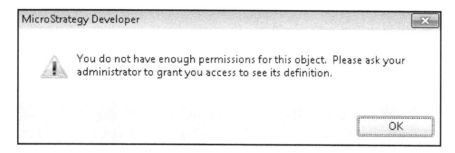

Or the option will simply be grayed out like **Edit** or **Delete**.

Permissions groups

The seven MicroStrategy permissions are grouped into four sets, listed as follows, that can be applied when editing an Object's ACL:

- **View**: Browse, read, use, and execute permissions granted
- **Modify**: Browse, read, write, delete, use, and execute permissions granted
- **Full Control**: All seven permissions granted
- **Denied All**: None of the seven permissions granted

An administrator can, however, apply a Custom set and turn on/off individual permissions.

Exercise – setting permissions

In this exercise, you will apply four different ACL to Reports. Take the following steps:

1. In MicroStrategy Developer, log in as **administrator** to the **MicroStrategy Analytics Modules** Project Source. First, we need to make sure our test subject, the User **smith** is not omnipotent within the **MicroStrategy Tutorial** Project. Therefore, it is necessary to make sure the **Bypass all object security access checks** privilege is not granted.

2. Edit the User **smith** | Change the **MicroStrategy Tutorial Security** Role to **Basic Access** (if you completed the previous exercise, it had **Admin Access** Security Role assigned) or, if you don't have this Security Role, select **Normal Users** | **OK**.

3. Browse to the **My Exercises** folder | Copy **My First Report** and paste it four times | Name each instance as follows:

- **My First Report (View)**
- **My First Report (Modify)**
- **My First Report (Full Control)**
- **My First Report (Denied All)**

4. Right-click on **My First Report (View)** | **Properties** | **Security** | select **Everyone** ACL entry and **Remove** | select **Public / Guest** ACL entry and **Remove**.

5. Click **Add** | Select the **Everyone** Group in the first dropdown | **Donald** (make sure the **Show users** check box is enabled) | Click on the funnel to reveal the User **smith** | Set **Access Permission** as **View**.

6. Repeat the process for the other three Reports by adding the **smith** ACL accordingly (Modify, Full Control, and so on). Make sure that both the **Everyone** and the **Public/Guest** ACL entries are removed on every Report.

The **Denied All** permission set is not available in the Access Permission dropdown when the User is added. Select any other permission set, such as View, and then change it on the Object's ACL, as follows:

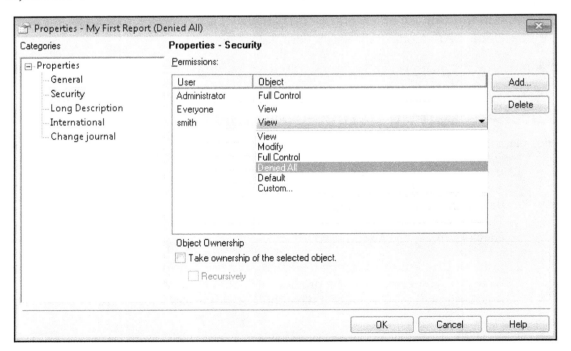

7. Log out from the **Administrator** session | Log in as the User **smith** | Browse to the **My Exercises** folder within the **MicroStrategy Tutorial**. Check that the following scenarios are true:

- **My First Report (View)**: Can be executed and opened in the Editor but not saved. It is also not possible to set the Object's ACL (**Properties** | **Security**).
- **My First Report (Modify)**: Can be executed and opened in the Editor, and saved, but it is not possible to set the Object's ACL (**Properties** | **Security**).
- **My First Report (Full Control)**: You can do all of the above plus set its ACL (**Properties** | **Security**).
- **My First Report (Denied All)**: The Report is not even visible.

8. This finalizes the exercise.

Data-level security

Data-level security in MicroStrategy is applied to the result set returned by Reports, Datasets, and Intelligent Cubes. The **Security Filter** is the Application Object responsible for enforcing this data-level security.

Limiting the data by user – Security Filters

Security Filters work similarly to regular Filters by adding a WHERE clause to the Report SQL.

The following is a quick reference table for a MicroStrategy Security Filter:

	1) What is it for?	To limit the data access based on a user profile
	2) What is it made of?	Attributes and Filters
	3) Where can it be used?	Users and User Groups

However, the following are key differences between Security Filters and regular Filters:

- Security Filters are tied to a User or User Group
- Security Filters are applied to every query that a User or User Group executes within a given Project
- Security Filters can only be created based on Attributes and not Metrics

Exercise – create and assign a Security Filter

In this exercise, you will create a Security Filter that will limit data for User **Smith** for a specific Region.

1. In MicroStrategy Developer, log in as **administrator** to the **MicroStrategy Analytics Modules** Project Source | **MicroStrategy Tutorial** | **My Exercises** folder.
2. Right-click | **New** | **Security Filter** | Browse for **Region** Attribute | Create a qualification with **Central** Region as the only element: (**Region In list Central**) | **Save and Close** | Name it **Central** Region.
3. Execute the previously created Report titled **Regional Revenue and Cost**, shown as follows:

	Metrics	Revenue	Cost
Region Call Center			
Central Milwaukee		$4,182,139	$3,544,594
Central Fargo		$847,227	$720,449
South New Orleans		$3,305,039	$2,800,048
South Memphis		$2,084,241	$1,782,276

4. Close the Report | Go to **Administrator** | **User Manager** | Edit the User **smith** | Go to **User Definition** on the left panel | **Security Filter** | select **MicroStrategy Tutorial** on the dropdown | **View** | **Security Filter Manager** window will open.
5. In the Security Filter Manager, you will have the option to manage, assign, or create new Security Filters. Browse to the **My Exercises** folder to locate the **Central** Region Security Filter | Double-click or move it to the right | **OK** to close the Security Filter Manager | **OK** to close the User Editor:

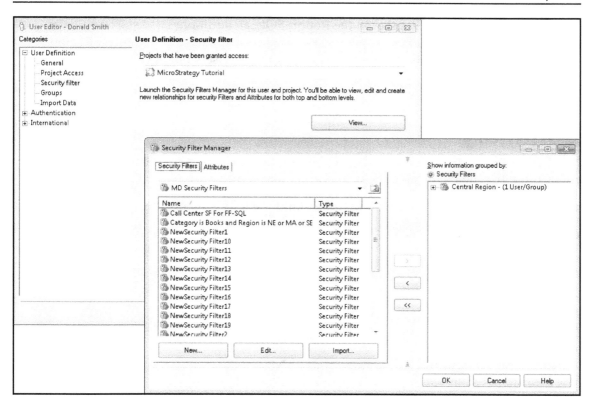

6. Log out from the **administrator** session | Log in as the User **smith** | Browse to the **My Exercises** folder within **MicroStrategy Tutorial** | Execute the previously created Report **Regional Revenue and Cost** | Notice how only Central Region data is returned, as shown in the following:

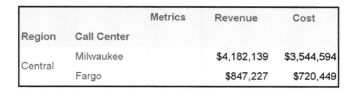

Region	Call Center	Metrics	Revenue	Cost
Central	Milwaukee		$4,182,139	$3,544,594
	Fargo		$847,227	$720,449

You can verify, that in the Report SQL, an additional `WHERE` condition is added: `[REGION_ID] in (4)`. This corresponds to the **Central** Region. This condition will not be applied to other Users but only to the User **smith**.

Summary

You have learned about MicroStrategy Configuration Objects in this chapter, specifically about those that helps MicroStrategy to set all three security levels.

You should also be able to create and understand the following objects:

Configuration Objects

- Users
- User Groups
- Security Roles

Application Objects

- Security Filters

The next chapter will not only conclude this book but also will cover additional Configuration Objects that allow automating Report and Intelligence Cubes execution. Also, we will learn about different Monitors that empower administrators to better manage and supervise the MicroStrategy environment and Projects.

Administration - Maintaining and Monitoring Your Project

7

The previous chapter introduced some MicroStrategy Configuration Objects that helped to create different levels of Security within the platform. We will now move on to our last topic, which also relates to Configuration Objects, but serving different purposes. The first set of objects allows administrators to establish connectivity with data sources while the second set controls how users subscribe to and refresh Reports and Intelligent Cubes. Next, we will explore some of MicroStrategy Developers' monitoring capabilities. The last pages of this book will be reserved for talking about the capabilities of three Administration tools: Object Manager, Integrity Manager, and Command Manager.

The following topics will be covered:

- Understanding which Configuration Objects are required to connect to a database
- Explaining what a MicroStrategy Database instance is and how to create it
- Explaining what a MicroStrategy Database connection is and how to create and associate it
- Explaining what a MicroStrategy Database login is and how to create and associate it
- Understanding what the MicroStrategy cache is
- Explaining what a MicroStrategy Schedule is and how to create it
- Explaining what a MicroStrategy Event is and how to create it
- Explaining what a MicroStrategy Subscription is and how to create it
- Understanding Object Manager's capabilities
- Understanding Integrity Manager's capabilities
- Understanding Command Manager's capabilities

Database connectivity in MicroStrategy

In Chapter 1, *Architecture - Installing and Configuring MicroStrategy,* we learned that MicroStrategy connects to its Metadata database either by configuring a 2-Tier (Direct) or a 3-Tier (Server) Project Source. However, we have not discussed yet how it connects to the source of the data. Each MicroStrategy Project can connect to one or multiple sources to which the generated SQL, resulting from Reports and Intelligent Cubes, gets executed. The following diagram depicts an example of how one Project connects to a database (for instance, a Data warehouse):

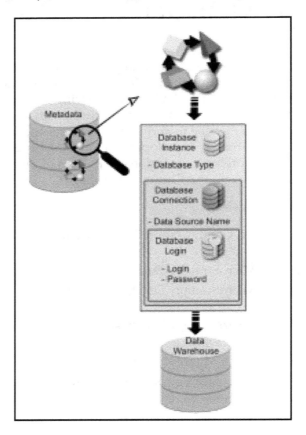

In the following sections, we will learn which MicroStrategy Objects are necessary to establish such connectivity.

Connecting to your source – Database Instances, Connections, and Logins

The MicroStrategy Database Instance is a Configuration Object, which logically represents a source database.

The following is a quick reference table for a MicroStrategy Database Instance:

	1) What is it for?	It is the logical representation of a Data warehouse or Data mart
	2) What is it made of?	Database type and Database Connection
	3) Where can it be used?	Projects

Database Instances are directly associated with MicroStrategy Projects. Each Project should have at least one Database Instance (Primary Database Instance), but it can also be configured with the Multisource option to connect to multiple relational data sources.

It is through this object that MicroStrategy can read tables and columns, and consequently import logical Tables into the MicroStrategy Schema. Database instances also define how and where the generated SQL will be executed.

The Database Instance contains two objects in addition to the database type. These objects are the Database Connection and Database Login.

A MicroStrategy Database Connection is necessary to associate the Database Instance to a Data Source Name (the DSN and a Login)

The following is a quick reference table for a MicroStrategy Database Connection:

	1) What is it for?	To establish connectivity with a database
	2) What is it made of?	DSN (Data Source Name ODBC) and Database Login
	3) Where can it be used?	Database Instance

The MicroStrategy Database Connection is a Configuration Object that defines the DSN to be used in the connection. To create a Database Connection through MicroStrategy Developer, the DSN should reside in the client machine to become available to the Database Connection editor.

The Database Connection contains one object in addition to the DSN. This object is the Database Login.

The following is a quick reference table for a MicroStrategy Database Login:

	1) What is it for?	To provide database user authentication
	2) What is it made of?	Database user login and password
	3) Where can it be used?	Database Connection

The MicroStrategy Database Login is also a Configuration Object that stores the username and password to connect to the data source.

Once the password is stored in the Database Login, it is not possible to read what string was typed into the object.

Exercise – Establish connectivity to a new database

In this exercise, you will establish connectivity to a new Microsoft Access database, creating a Database Instance, Database Connection, and Database Login:

You will need Microsoft Access installed to create a new database.

1. Create a new Microsoft Access database. Add a dummy table. Name both the database and the table `Chapter7`.

If you don't know how to create a MS Access database, simply right-click on the Data Explorer in the machine where it is installed | **New** | **Microsoft Access Database**.

2. For this exercise, we will use an MS Access 2000 file with the *.mdb. If your machine has an MS Access driver for .accdb, you can use such a file. We will learn in the following step how to add a DSN and verify which MS Access drivers are installed in your machine. To change a *.accdb file to *.mdb, open the Microsoft Access database, click on **File** | **Save As** | **Access 2000 Database(*.mdb)**:

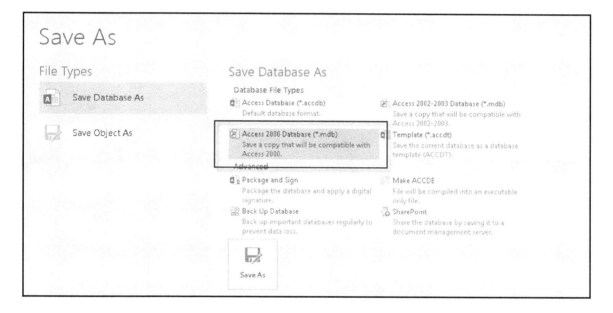

3. Create a System DSN: Open the **32-bit ODBC Administrator** or **ODBC Data Sources (32-bit)** depending on your Windows OS version (you can use the Windows search option to locate it). The System DSN is the second tab:

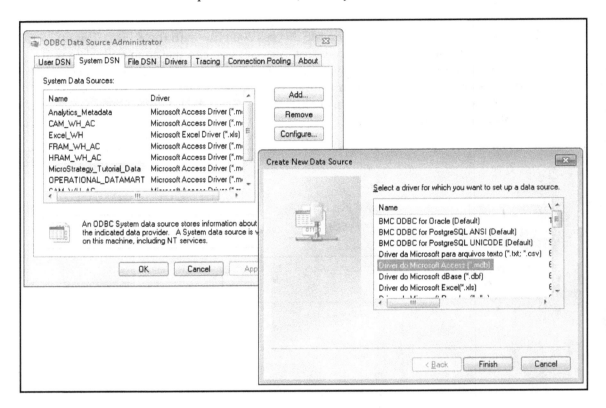

In this exercise, we use 32-bit, since we utilize an MS Access database. Check with your Database Administrator on how to create the DSN for your specific database type, version, and environment.

4. Click **Add** and locate **Driver do Microsoft Access (*.mdb)** or **Microsoft Access Driver (*.mdb)** | **Finish**.

You might also have a newer version of the MS Access driver, such as Microsoft Access Driver (*.mdb, *.accdb)

5. For the Data Source Name, type `Chapter7DSN` | **Database** | **Select…** | Locate your **Chapter7.mdb** (or `.accdb`) file on your machine | **OK**. You should be able to see the DSN listed under the **System DSN** tab | **OK** to exit the **ODBC Data Source Administrator**.

6. In MicroStrategy Developer, log in to the **MicroStrategy Analytics Modules** Project Source.

7. Open **Administration** | **Configuration Managers** | **Database Instances** and right-click then choose **New** | **Database Instance**. The editor will open.

8. For the **Database instance name**, type `Chapter7DBI`. In the **Database connection type** dropdown, locate your MS Access version; for this exercise, it is **Microsoft Access 2007**. Don't close the Database Instance editor yet:

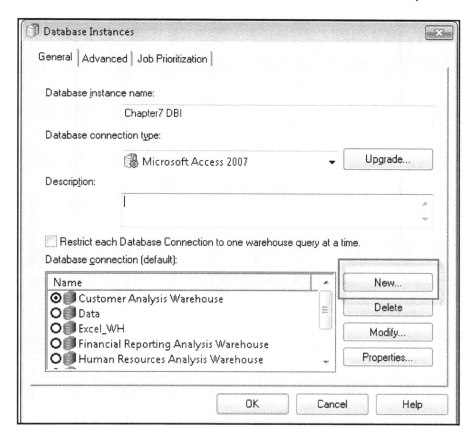

9. We will create a MicroStrategy Database Connection within the Database Instance. Click **New** in the Database Instance editor on the **Database connection (default)** section | The Database Connection editor will open | for **Database connection name**, type Chapter7DBC. Locate in the **Local system ODBC data sources** list the DSN you created in previous steps, **Chapter7DSN**, and select the radio button. Don't close the Database Connection editor yet.

10. We will create a MicroStrategy Database Login within the Database Connection. Click **New** in the Database Connection editor, in the Database login name section | The Database Login editor will open | for **Database login**, type Chapter7DBL | Under **Login ID** type Administrator and **Password:** <blank> (for MS Access, it doesn't matter what you type unless you have specified login credentials) | **OK**:

11. Before closing the Database Connection editor, make sure both the **Chapter7DL** Database Login and the **Chapter7DSN Local system ODBC data source** are selected:

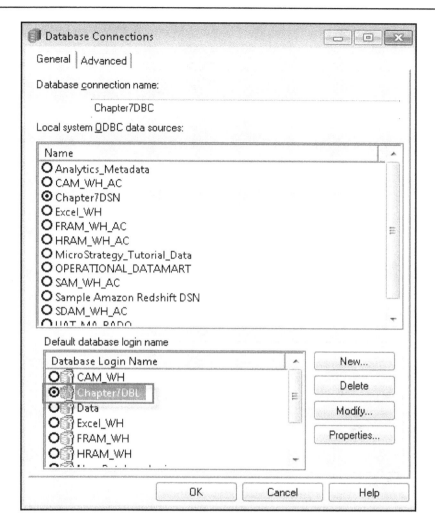

By default, MicroStrategy will not select the radio button for the newly created object, so you need to double-check everything is correct before closing the editor.

12. Click **OK** to close the Database Connection editor | You might see a warning message mentioning that, on a 3-Tier connection, the Intelligence Server must be restarted, while on a 2-Tier connection, the Projects need to be reloaded (connected and disconnected) for changes to take effect; click **OK**. Before closing the Database Instance editor, make sure the **Chapter7DC** Database Connection is selected:

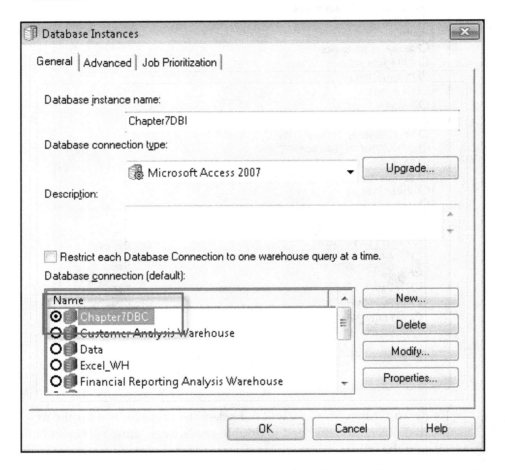

13. Click **OK** to close the Database Instance editor | You will see your newly created Database Instance in the **Configuration Manager**.
14. We will now test the connection by creating a new Project and associating it with the Database Instance. Go to **Schema** | **Create New Project** | **Create project** ; name it Chapter7 and leave the defaults, click **OK**, and wait until the Project is created.

15. Click on **Select tables from Warehouse Catalog** | Select **Chapter7DBI** in the dropdown | **OK** | The Warehouse Catalog should open and your test table **Chapter7** should be there. You can right-click on the table and see its **Table Structure** to double-check it is the one you created Click **Save and Close** then **OK** to close the Project creation assistant.

16. This finalizes the exercise.

Improving Reporting Performance – MicroStrategy Cache

When a Report is executed, it goes through the cycle we described in Chapter 1, *Architecture - Installing and Configuring MicroStrategy,* (Refer to Intelligent Server Engines): SQL Generation-Query Execution-Results format and Crosstab. However, for both complex Reports and very large Result sets, this process could take time and resources each time the Report is executed. For scenarios where ad hoc reporting is not needed, the result set from a previously executed Report can be stored in what MicroStrategy calls a cache. When a user executes a Report, a cache is created within a file and the Intelligence Server loads the result set into its memory. Report caching can be enabled either at the Project level or at the Report level.

> Ad hoc reporting involves Reports that require users to answer one or more Prompts. These are sometimes also known as OLAP Reports.

There are two other objects that generate caches too: Intelligent Cubes and Documents.

Intelligent Cube caches are a more optimal form of regular Report caches. Intelligent Cubes can basically serve as a cache for different Reports. For example, let's imagine there is a prompted Report that asks the user for a Region. If you want to create a Report cache, you will need more than one cached result set, such as one for each Region (this is why the Report cache is usually not enabled for prompted/ad hoc reports). On the other hand, with an Intelligent Cube, you could just cache the result set for all Regions and then associate a prompted Region Report to the Cube.

Finally, Document caches can be enabled on different formats such as Excel, HTML, PDF, and XML. The first three formats are used for exporting purposes, while the XML is used in MicroStrategy web visualization modes (Express Mode and Interactive).

The following sections describe which MicroStrategy Configuration objects are used to refresh these caches.

Automating tasks – Schedules

A MicroStrategy Schedule is a Configuration Object that allows MicroStrategy to program a cache and Intelligent Cube refresh and administration tasks such as cache deletion, Project loading, history list purging, and statistics purging, and so on.

The following is a quick reference table for a MicroStrategy Schedule:

	1) What is it for?	To automate administration tasks such as reports and Intelligent Cubes execution
	2) What is it made of?	Time-based, Events
	3) Where can it be used?	Subscriptions

Schedules can be either time-based or event-based. Time-based Schedules define frequency based on a calendar, date, and times, whereas event-based Schedules need an additional object to be triggered. This object is a MicroStrategy Event, discussed in the next section.

Defining Triggers – Events

A MicroStrategy Event is a Configuration Object representing an external action that should trigger a Schedule in MicroStrategy. An example of such an action could be data loading in a source table.

The following is a quick reference table for a MicroStrategy Event:

	1) What is it for?	To trigger an event-based Schedule
	2) What is it made of?	Event name
	3) Where can it be used?	Schedules

While any event could be triggered manually in MicroStrategy Developer, it makes more sense to call it externally with a scripting tool such as Command Manager. We will learn more about this application later.

Refreshing your data – Subscriptions

Administrators and developers can define when and how cached Reports and Intelligent Cubes should be refreshed. However, we can empower final users by associating them to existing Schedules. When a Schedule is associated to refresh a cached Report or Intelligent Cube, a new object is created: a MicroStrategy Subscription.

The following is a quick reference table for a MicroStrategy Subscription:

	1) What is it for?	To associate a Schedule with a Report/ Intelligent Cube refresh or administration task
	2) What is it made of?	Schedules
	3) Where can it be used?	N/a

Users can subscribe their Reports and Intelligent Cubes using MicroStrategy Web/Mobile or MicroStrategy Developer.

Exercise – Subscribing your Reports

This exercise will have three parts. In the first part, you will create an Event and then associate (subscribe) it to a Schedule to trigger a Report. The second part will consist of creating another Subscription, but to refresh an Intelligent Cube.

The last part will consist of creating a Schedule, but time-based, and then a Subscription in MicroStrategy Web:

1. In MicroStrategy Developer, log in to the **MicroStrategy Analytics Modules** Project Source.
2. Open **Administration** | **Configuration Managers** | **Events** | Right-click | **New** | **Event** | Name it `TableLoad`.

As you can see, the Event is a simple object that only consists of its name.

3. Open **Administration** | **Configuration Managers** | **Schedules** | Right-click | **New** | **Schedule** | Name it `On table load`.
4. Select **Event-triggered** | **Next**:

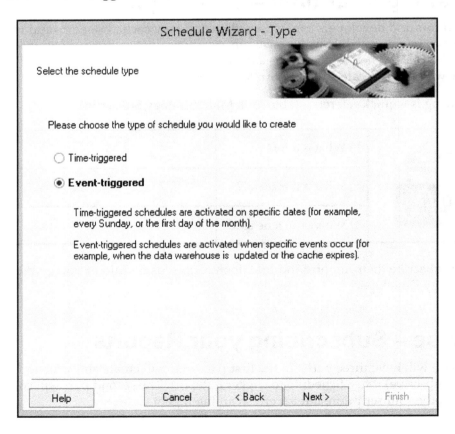

6. You can decide when each Schedule starts its validity period and if it expires on a given date. Leave the default **Start** and **End by** dates, and then **Next**.

7. Select the radio button corresponding to the **TableLoad** Event | **Finish** | Verify that your newly created Schedule is available under **Configuration Managers** | **Schedules**.

8. Go to the **My Exercises** folder within **MicroStrategy Tutorial** Project | Edit **My First Report** | **Data** Menu | **Report Caching Options** | You should see this window:

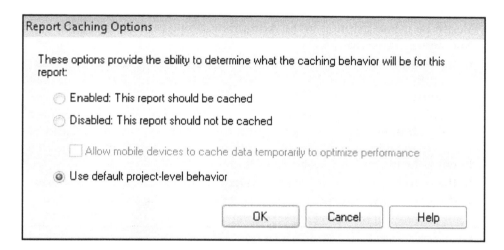

 You can control the caching behavior of any given Report. By default, a Report uses the Project level definition, which is overwritten by the Report level one.

9. Select **Enabled: This report should be cached** | **OK** | Don't execute the Report yet, just click **Save and Close**.

 For the next steps, you will need to connect to a Server Project Source (3-Tier) and have MicroStrategy OLAP Services installed/licensed.

10. Connect to **MicroStrategy Analytics Modules** in 3-Tier mode (you will need to configure the Intelligence Server to point to the corresponding Metadata; for reference, check Chapter 1, *Architecture - Installing and Configuring MicroStrategy*).

11. Go to the **My Exercises** folder within **MicroStrategy Tutorial** Project | Right-click on **My First Report** | **Schedule Delivery to** | **Update Cache**.

In this step, you are creating a Subscription to update the Report's cache.

12. Name it **Table Load Subscription** | Select the **On table load** Schedule from the dropdown | Leave the default settings | **OK**.

13. Verify your Subscription in the **Administration** tree, **Configuration Managers>Subscriptions**.

14. In the **Administration** tree, go to **System Monitors** | **Caches** | **Reports** | **MicroStrategy Tutorial** | No cache should be there; if there is one, select it with the mouse and delete it.

15. We will manually trigger the Event so that the Report cache gets created. In the **Administration** tree, go to **Configuration Managers** | **Events** | **TableLoad** Event, then right-click | **Trigger** | You will see a window indicating that the Event got triggered successfully | **OK**.

16. In the **Administration** tree, go to **System Monitors** | **Caches** | **Reports** | **MicroStrategy Tutorial** | Your newly created cache should be there:

Report Na... ▽	Project Name	Status	Last Update	Cache Si...	Expiration	Type	Cache ID
My First Report	MicroStrategy Tutorial	R, L, U, F	9/13/2018 11:00:56 PM	26	9/14/2018 11:00:56 PM	Matching	8BA3846C11E8B7E3F3B00080EFA53FC3

17. We will move on to the second part of this exercise. Go to the **My Exercises** folder within the **MicroStrategy Tutorial** Project | Right-click | **New** | **Intelligent Cube** | Add **Month** and **Region** Attributes, **Revenue** and **Cost** Metrics | **Save and Close** | Name it **Simple Cube**.

Don't execute it yet, since it will create a cache.

18. Right-click **Simple Cube** | **Schedule Delivery to** | **Refresh Cube** | Name it **Refresh Cube** | Select the **On table load** Schedule from the dropdown | Leave the default settings | **OK**.

19. Manually trigger the **TableLoad** Event. In the **Administration** tree, go to **Configuration Managers** | **Events** | **TableLoad** Event. Right-click | **Trigger** | You will see a window indicating that the Event got triggered successfully | **OK**.

 Note that every Subscription using the same Event will be triggered. In our exercise, this means one Report cache and one Intelligent Cube. If you don't want this behavior, then separate Events and Schedules must be created.

20. To verify your Intelligent Cube refresh, go to the **Administration** tree | **System Monitors** | **Caches** | **Intelligent Cubes** | Your refreshed cube should be there:

Intelligent Cube Report Name	Project Name	Status	Last Update Time	Hit Count	Size (KB)	Owner
Simple Cube	MicroStrategy Tutorial	A, L, F	9/13/2018 11:12:39 PM	0	273	Administrator

21. We will create a time-based Schedule. Open the **Administration** Tree | **Configuration Managers** | **Schedules** | Right-click | **New** | **Schedule** | Name it **Daily 6am** | **Next** and select **Time-triggered** | Leave the default **Start** and **End by dates** | **Next** | For **Recurrence pattern**, select **Daily, Every 1 day(s)** | **Time to trigger**, and set it to execute at 6:00 AM:

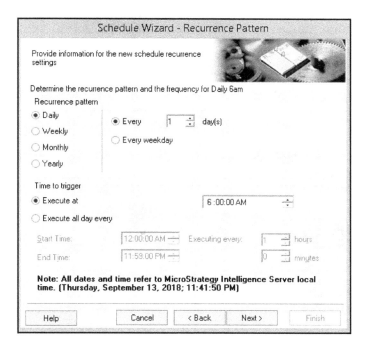

Take time to review the available options, which allow administrators to set up flexible and dynamic schedules.

22. Click **Next** | Review the next dates and times on which this Schedule will run | **Finish**.
23. For the last part of the exercise, you will need to connect to **MicroStrategy Tutorial** through MicroStrategy Web | Execute M**y First Report** in the **My Exercises** folder | Once the Report is executed, go to the **Report Home** menu | **Subscribe to** | **Cache Update**.

 If MicroStrategy Distribution Services are configured, the user can select to subscribe the Report to other delivery methods such as e-mail, file, or printer. Also, if MicroStrategy Mobile is set up, the Report can be delivered to the mobile app.

24. Similar to MicroStrategy Developer, add a name to the Subscription: **My Web Subscription** | Associate it to **Daily 6am** Schedule | **OK**.
25. Navigate to the **My Exercises** folder and hover over **My First Report**. You will see the following options:

26. Click on **Subscriptions** and verify that your newly created Subscription is there under Cache Update.
27. This finalizes the exercise.

Monitoring your Project – MicroStrategy Developer Monitors

This section will cover some of MicroStrategy Developer's monitoring capabilities. Under MicroStrategy Developer's **Administrator** tree, there is a branch called **System Monitors**. A Project Source configured as Direct or 2-Tier will not feature in these, since it is necessary the Intelligence Server to enable these monitors, hence a 3-Tier configuration is required.

To use System Monitors, the MicroStrategy User must have the corresponding privilege to access that monitor (such as Jobs Monitor or Caches Monitor, and so on).

Jobs Monitor

MicroStrategy Job Monitor displays jobs that are currently executing in the Intelligent Server. Once a job completes, it will no longer be visible. You can see the Job ID, the User that submitted it, status (executing, waiting in queue, waiting for autoprompt, canceling, and so on), report/document name, and Project.

Useful tips

The following are some of the useful tips for Jobs Monitor:

- To refresh the Job Monitor, press *F5*. There is no auto-refresh built into the monitor.
- To view a job's details, such as SQL, double-click to access the **Quick View** for that job.
- To cancel a job, right-click and choose **Cancel Job** (or press *Delete*).

User Connections Monitor

MicroStrategy User Connections Monitor displays all users connected to projects. There are at least two connections per User, one listed as **<Server>**, which indicates a connection to the Project Source, and one for each of the projects the User is connected to.

Useful tips

The following are some of the useful tips for User Connections Monitor:

- To view User connection details, double-click to access **Quick View**
- To disconnect a User, right-click and choose **Disconnect** (or *Delete*)
- If the **<Server>** connection is disconnected, any projects that the User was connected to will be disconnected as well

Database Connections Monitor

MicroStrategy Database Connections Monitor shows all Busy and Cached connections to databases. There are two types of connections shown:

- **Connections to the Metadata**: Shown as **<Repository Connection>**, they are opened when the User accesses any Project, even if they don't execute any Reports.
- **Connections to the source database**: Shown as **<Database Instance name>**, they are opened any time a non-cached Report or Intelligent Cube is executed or non-cached elements are browsed. These connections can also be as follows:
  - **Busy**: This status is shown when the connection is processing a job.
  - **Cached**: This status is shown when the job processing has been completed. A cached database connection can then be re-utilized to process new job requests to the same database since it remains open.

 There are some scenarios when the connection to the source database won't be cached. For example, when a connection surpasses the Database Connection timeout governors, if a Report/Intelligent Cube uses a pre or post SQL statement, any user-defined SQL, Freeform SQL Reports, or Data mart Objects.

Useful tips

The following are some of the useful tips for Database Connections Monitor:

- To view connection details, double-click to access **Quick View**
- To delete a database connection, right-click and choose **Disconnect** (or DEL)

Caches Monitor

MicroStrategy Caches shows result caches from Reports, Documents, and Intelligent Cubes.

Operations for Caches

An administrative User can perform the following operations over caches:

- **Delete**: Removes the cache from memory and the file from disk
- **Invalidate**: Voids the cache, but any User with a History List message pointed to it will remain active

 A History List message is a shortcut to a Report's result set that can be retrieved at any time, without having to re-execute the Report. It can be created in Developer by right-clicking on a Report | **Send to History**. In MicroStrategy Web, an executed Report can be sent to the History list by opening the **Report Home** menu | **Add to History List**.

- **Load from disk**: Loads into the Intelligent Server memory a file-based cache that has been previously unloaded from it.
- **Unload to disk**: Stores to disk a cache that resides in the Intelligent Server memory.

Operations for Intelligent Cubes

- **Delete:** Removes the Intelligent Cube from memory and the file from disk. This action will not remove the Intelligent Cube from the Metadata/Project.
- **Unload from memory**: Moves the Intelligent Cube from the server's memory to disk.
- **Load in memory**: Moves the Intelligent Cube from disk to the server's memory.

MicroStrategy Administrative Clients

The last section of this book will briefly describe three MicroStrategy tools for Administration and Project Maintenance: Command Manager, Object Manager, and Integrity Manager.

 There are additional tools to help Administrators to configure, monitor, and automate the MicroStrategy platform, such as Enterprise Manager, Operations Manager, and System Manager. However, these are out of the scope of this book. For information about these, you can search in the MicroStrategy Community Portal: https://community.microstrategy.com.

Migrating your Objects – Object Manager

A MicroStrategy Project lifecycle usually starts from gathering requirements from the business, investigating whether the organization's source systems have data that could satisfy such requirements, and then moving on to designing a data model that supports them, building a database schema to host the data from the source systems, and finally developing MicroStrategy objects from that schema. It is recommended at least two MicroStrategy environments: DEV (developing environment) where the objects are built and PROD (production environment) where the users consume the developed Reports and Documents. However, it is best practice to have an additional environment to do unit, system, and/or performance testing and perform user acceptance testing (UAT), which marks the objects ready to be deployed into PROD. These objects need to be moved from one Project to the other while their DEV-TEST-ACCEPT-PROD cycle advances. MicroStrategy Object Manager is the Administrative tool that helps migrate these objects across Projects.

Comparing your Reports – Integrity Manager

There are some scenarios in which developers or administrators need to compare Reports within or across Projects to ensure the integrity of both data and the underlying SQL to generate it. Examples of these include once objects are migrated from one Project to another, if Project Duplication occurs and some changes are performed to objects, or if a source database (for example, a data warehouse) has been updated or upgraded. MicroStrategy Integrity Manager is a tool that helps to compare the SQL generated by a Report and the data returned as a result of its execution side by side.

Automating Scripts – Command Manager

Sometimes, it is necessary to perform a large number of changes to MicroStrategy objects, for example, User creation or cache invalidation. In other scenarios, there might be the need to call MicroStrategy commands from a third-party scheduling tool such as BMC Control-M. MicroStrategy Command Manager allows administrators to execute text commands or scripts to perform and automate application and administrative tasks in batches. It also allows scheduling tools such as BMC Control-M or Airlfow Scheduler to trigger MicroStrategy commands, for example, to refresh Intelligent Cubes or trigger MicroStrategy Events.

Exercise – Using Command, Object, and Integrity Managers

In this exercise, you will use Command Manager to create a Project, then Object Manager to move some objects into it. Finally, Integrity Manager will be used to compare the Reports between source and target Projects:

1. Open MicroStrategy Command Manager. In Windows, it is installed by default in C:\ProgramData\Microsoft\Windows\Start Menu\Programs\MicroStrategy Products.

2. Connect to the **MicroStrategy Analytics Modules** Project Source. If the Login window doesn't open by default, go to **File** | **Connect** | **MicroStrategy Metadata**.

3. We will now check the different outlines (scripts and examples) that exist in Command Manager. Click on the **Outlines...** button:

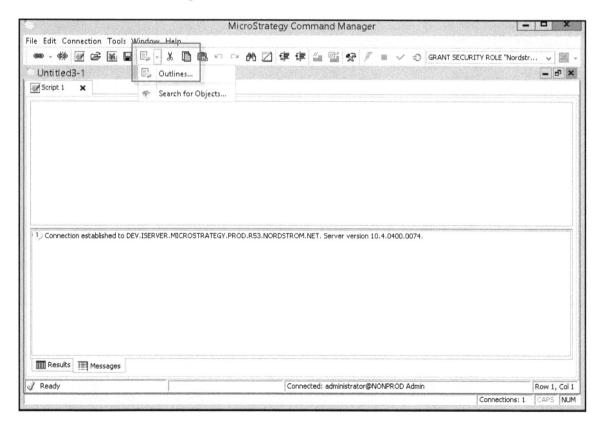

From the Outlines window, **Choose Outline** contains commands for different object types and administrative tasks. Give yourself a few minutes to browse through the different folders and familiarize yourself with the examples and syntax.

4. We will first list all the Reports we have created so far within MicroStrategy Tutorial. Open the **Report_Outlines** folder | **List_Reports_Outline** | Verify the syntax and review the sample | **Insert** | **Cancel** to close the window:

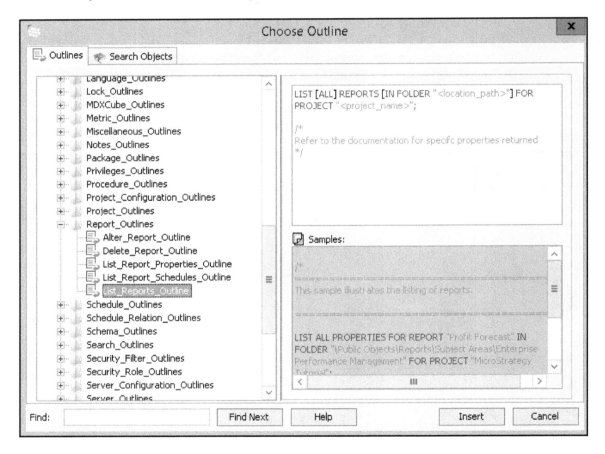

5. Modify the script so that it reads like this:

```
LIST ALL REPORTS IN FOLDER "\Public Objects\Reports\My
Exercises" FOR PROJECT "MicroStrategy Tutorial";
```

Make sure that the folder path starts with \. If you saved your Reports in a different path, change the command accordingly.

6. Click on the Execute icon to run the command:

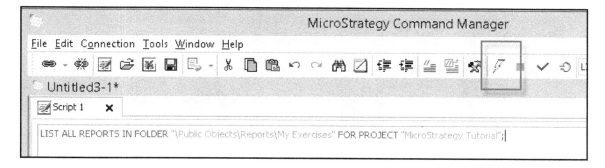

You should see all Reports and Intelligent Cubes within that folder.

7. We will create a new Project. Delete the prior script and click on **Insert Outline** | **Project_Outlines** | **Create_Project_Outline** | **Insert** | Close the window.

8. Modify the script so that it reads like this:

```
CREATE PROJECT "MicroStrategy Tutorial UAT" DESCRIPTION "User
Acceptance Project";
```

9. Click on the Execute icon to run the command.

10. In MicroStrategy Developer, reconnect to the **MicroStrategy Analytics Modules** Project Source. If it was opened, close and reopen it. Make sure that your newly created Project **MicroStrategy Tutorial UAT** is there.

This is an empty Project with no objects, but with the default folder structure. Also, there is no Database instance associated to it. If you want to move Reports from MicroStrategy Tutorial, which uses a source database, we will need to associate the same database instance to the MicroStrategy Tutorial UAT Project. For this exercise, this won't be required since we will use the Intelligent Cube imported from an Excel file in Chapter 5, *Dashboarding - Creating Visual Reporting*, which won't connect to the database.

11. We will use Object Manager to move some objects into the new Project. Open MicroStrategy Object Manager. In Windows, it is installed by default in
    `C:\ProgramData\Microsoft\Windows\Start`
    `Menu\Programs\MicroStrategy Products.`

12. In the **Open Project Source** window, select **MicroStrategy Analytics Modules** Project Source and click **OPEN**.

You can either select a 2-Tier or 3-Tier Project Source.

13. Click on **File** | **Open** | This will open a second window to the same **MicroStrategy Analytics Modules Project** Source | **OPEN**.

This step is optional since you can move the objects within the same Project Source/window.

14. There will be two windows on your screen. Let's arrange them horizontally. Select **Window** | **Tile Horizontally**.

15. In the top window, browse in **MicroStrategy Tutorial** and locate **My Exercises**. In the lower window, browse in **MicroStrategy Tutorial UAT** to **\Public Objects\Reports**.

16. Drag and drop the following objects from **MicroStrategy Tutorial** to the **Reports** folder in **MicroStrategy Tutorial UAT**:

    • Imported Cube
    • Category Dataset

A **Conflict Resolution** window will open. There, you can see which objects will be moved and the **Action** associated with the migration, such as **Use Existing, Replace, Use Newer,** or **Create New**. In this example, the two objects are new to the Project. Click **Proceed** to move the objects to the new Project.

Every time any Schema Objects are moved to a Project, it is necessary to perform an Update Schema: In **Object Manager Project** menu | Update **Schema**. In this exercise, this is not necessary.

17. Close each Project source by right-clicking the Project Source in Object Manager | **Disconnect from Project Source** | Close Object Manager.

18. Open MicroStrategy Web to publish the Intelligent Cube in the new Project and test our Report. Open **MicroStrategy Tutorial UAT Project** and navigate to **Shared Reports**; there you will see the two objects we moved | Right-click **Imported Cube** | **Republish**. Browse to the folder in your computer where the TutorialData.xlsx file is and select it | **Open** | **Finish**.

19. Once the cube is refreshed, click **Done** | Execute the **Category Dataset** Report.

20. The last part of this exercise consists of verifying the two reports are the same between both environments. This last part requires a Server connection/3-Tier Project Source. Open MicroStrategy Integrity Manager. In Windows, it is installed by default in C:\ProgramData\Microsoft\Windows\Start Menu\Programs\MicroStrategy Products.

21. Go to **File** | **Create Test** | **Project versus Project**.

You might want to review the different options for future reference.

22. In the **Server Name** box, type the Intelligent Server name. If you don't know or you can't remember its name, you can go to MicroStrategy Developer and right-click on the Project Source | **Modify Project Source** | Copy the Server name from the Project Source Manager box | Switch to Integrity Manager and paste it in | Input the Port number (you can use the same procedure as before) | Type the **Login id** and **Password** | Select **MicroStrategy Tutorial** from the Project dropdown | **Next**.

23. Repeat the process to add a MicroStrategy Tutorial UAT Project | **Next** | the MicroStrategy Tutorial folder structure will be shown. Browse to the **My Exercises** folder and select **Category Dataset** | **Next** | **Next** (leave the text boxes about prompt answers blank) | **Next** (leave the default output directory for log files) | Check **SQL/MDX** and **Data** | **Next:**

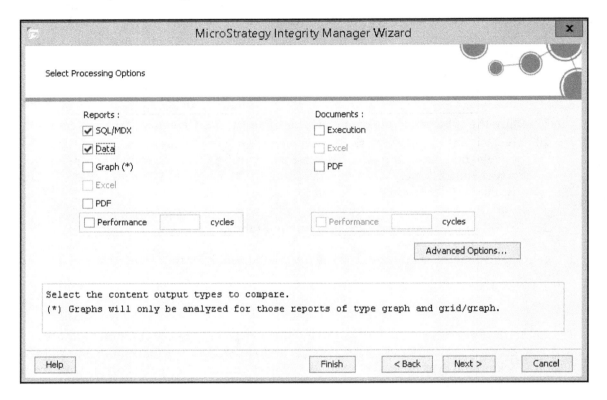

24. Click **Save Test** | **Filename Chapter7** | **Save** | **Run** | Select the **Category Dataset** row to see the results | Check that both **SQL/MDX** and **Data** tabs match:

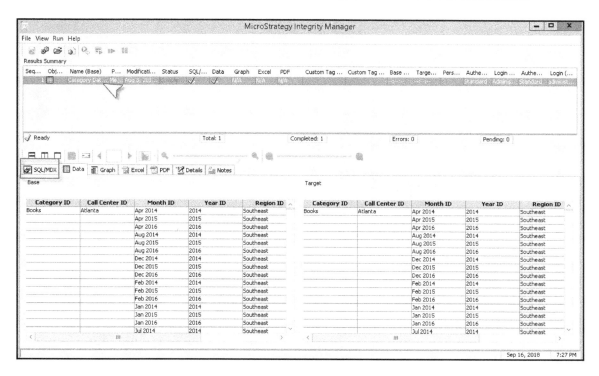

 In this example, we are not really using SQL since the Report accesses a cube imported from an Excel file.

25. Without closing Integrity Manager, go back to MicroStrategy Developer | Access the **MicroStrategy Tutorial UAT** Project | locate the **Category Dataset** Report | **Edit** | Remove **Month** from the Report view | **Save and Close.**

26. Return to Integrity Manager | Select the **Category Dataset** row | Right-click **Refresh Selected Items** to rerun the test | Select the **Category Dataset** row to see the results | Verify that the **SQL/MDX** and **Data** tabs do not match:

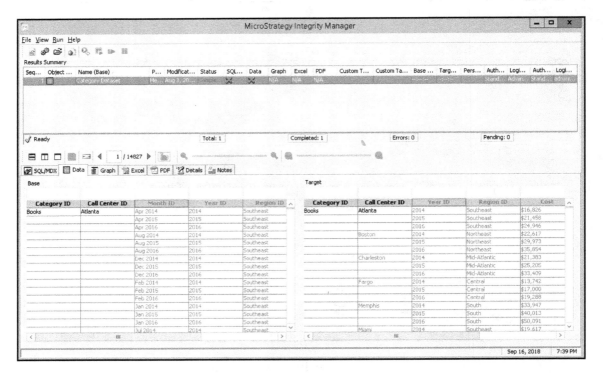

27. This finalizes the exercise.

Summary

This final chapter introduced the Configuration objects used to establish connectivity to source databases from MicroStrategy Projects. Also, we learned about MicroStrategy caches and how to automatically refresh them through Subscriptions. We covered the following Configuration Objects:

- Database Instance
- Database Connection
- Database Login
- Schedule
- Event
- Subscription

The second part of this chapter was used to explain some of the main MicroStrategy Developer monitors and their capabilities. At the end of the chapter, three Administrator tools where described: Command Manager, Object Manager, and Integrity Manager.

Quick Reference Tables by Object Type

Schema Objects

Tables

	1) What is it for?	To map fields to a physical table or view in a database. To create MicroStrategy expressions
	2) What is it made of?	Columns and data types
	3) Where can it be used?	Attributes, Facts and Transformations

Attributes

	1) What is it for?	To map business contexts to a column in a look up table. To give context to business measures (facts)
	2) What is it made of?	Columns from a MicroStrategy Table (Attribute Forms)
	3) Where can it be used?	Hierarchies, Templates, Reports, Filters, Metrics, Prompts, Drill Maps

Facts

	1) What is it for?	To map business measures to a column or columns in a fact table
	2) What is it made of?	Columns from a MicroStrategy Table (Expressions)
	3) Where can it be used?	Metrics, Object Prompts, Base Formulas

Hierarchies

	1) What is it for?	To visualize Attributes, their elements and relationships. To define Drill Maps.
	2) What is it made of?	Attributes
	3) Where can it be used?	Drill Maps, Templates and Metrics (in its dimensionality)

Transformations

	1) What is it for?	To compare measures across time
	2) What is it made of?	Columns from a MicroStrategy Table (Expression-based/Table-based)
	3) Where can it be used?	Metrics

Application / Public Objects

Templates

	1) What is it for?	To layout and format the information in the Report
	2) What is it made of?	Attributes, Metrics, Consolidations, Custom Groups, Object Prompts
	3) Where can it be used?	Reports, Object Prompts, Drill Maps

Filters

	1) What is it for?	To slice and segment the information
	2) What is it made of?	Attributes, Metrics, other Filters, Prompts, Reports and Expressions
	3) Where can it be used?	Reports, Filters, Metrics, Custom Groups, Object Prompts, Hierarchies

Metrics

	1) What is it for?	To aggregate a business measure (Fact) into a business context (Attribute)
	2) What is it made of?	Functions and Operators, Facts, Attributes, other Metrics, Base Formulas, Filters, Transformations, Subtotals
	3) Where can it be used?	Templates, Filters, Object Prompts and other Metrics

Reports

	1) What is it for?	To visualize, manipulate, analyze and discover information
	2) What is it made of?	Filters and Templates
	3) Where can it be used?	Documents, Filters and another Reports

Prompts

	1) What is it for?	To gather information from the user and create dynamic queries for a Report
	2) What is it made of?	Filters, Attributes, Hierarchies Metrics, Templates, Facts, Metrics, Functions, Reports, Custom Groups, Consolidations, Values
	3) Where can it be used?	Reports, Filters, Metrics, Custom Groups, Prompts, Templates, Subtotals

Custom Groups

	1) What is it for?	To create dynamic sets of data with different filtering criteria
	2) What is it made of?	Custom Group elements (Filters and Bands or N-tiles)
	3) Where can it be used?	Templates, Object Prompts, Drill Maps

Consolidations

	1) What is it for?	To create static or derived sets of data based on Attribute elements
	2) What is it made of?	Consolidation elements (from Attribute Elements)
	3) Where can it be used?	Templates, Object Prompts, Drill Maps

Drill Maps

	1) What is it for?	To define drill paths or routes to discover information at a different level
	2) What is it made of?	Drill Paths (Attributes, Hierarchies and Templates)
	3) Where can it be used?	Reports, Templates, Projects

Intelligent Cubes

	1) What is it for?	To create an in-memory data sources
	2) What is it made of?	Filters and Template, Reports
	3) Where can it be used?	Documents, Reports (Data set)

Documents

	1) What is it for?	To create Enterprise certified ("official") Dashboards and interactive data visualizations
	2) What is it made of?	Reports, Datasets, Intelligent Cubes
	3) Where can it be used?	N/a (It is the largest Public Object)

Dashboards (former Visual Insight Object)

	1) What is it for?	To create self-service Dashboards and interactive data visualizations
	2) What is it made of?	Reports, Datasets, Intelligent Cubes
	3) Where can it be used?	N/a (It is the largest Public Object)

Configuration Objects

Projects

	1) What is it for?	To contain other objects grouped by business affinity
	2) What is it made of?	All Public and Schema Objects
	3) Where can it be used?	N/a. This is the "largest" object in the metadata

Users

	1) What is it for?	To represent user profiles
	2) What is it made of?	Authentication type, privileges, Security Roles, Security Filters
	3) Where can it be used?	User Groups

Groups

	1) What is it for?	To create sets of users with similar profiles
	2) What is it made of?	Authentication type, privileges, Security Roles, Security Filters, Users, User Groups (Subgroups)
	3) Where can it be used?	User Groups

Security Roles

	1) What is it for?	To create sets of privileges
	2) What is it made of?	Privileges
	3) Where can it be used?	Users and User Groups

Database Instance

	1) What is it for?	It is the logical representation of a Data warehouse or Data mart
	2) What is it made of?	Database type and Database Connection
	3) Where can it be used?	Projects

Database Connection

	1) What is it for?	To establish connectivity with a database
	2) What is it made of?	DSN (Data Source Name ODBC) and Database Login
	3) Where can it be used?	Database Instance

Database Login

	1) What is it for?	To provide database user authentication
	2) What is it made of?	Database user login and password
	3) Where can it be used?	Database Connection

Events

	1) What is it for?	To trigger an event-based Schedule
	2) What is it made of?	Event name
	3) Where can it be used?	Schedules

Schedules

	1) What is it for?	To automate administration tasks such as reports and Intelligent Cubes execution
	2) What is it made of?	Time-based, Events
	3) Where can it be used?	Subscriptions

Subscriptions

	1) What is it for?	To associate a Schedule with a Report/ Intelligent Cube refresh or administration task
	2) What is it made of?	Schedules
	3) Where can it be used?	N/a

Security Filters

	1) What is it for?	To limit the data access based on a user profile
	2) What is it made of?	Attributes and Filters
	3) Where can it be used?	Users and User Groups

Other Books You May Enjoy

If you enjoyed this book, you may be interested in these other books by Packt:

Mastering Tableau
David Baldwin

ISBN: 9781784397692

- Create a worksheet that can display the current balance for any given period in time
- Recreate a star schema from in a data warehouse in Tableau
- Combine level of detail calculations with table calculations, sets, and parameters
- Create custom polygons to build filled maps for area codes in the USA
- Visualize data using a set of analytical and advanced charting techniques
- Know when to use Tableau instead of PowerPoint
- Build a dashboard and export it to PowerPoint

Microsoft Power BI Cookbook
Brett Powell

ISBN: 9781788290142

- Cleanse, stage, and integrate your data sources with Power BI
- Abstract data complexities and provide users with intuitive, self-service BI capabilities
- Build business logic and analysis into your solutions via the DAX programming language and dynamic, dashboard-ready calculations
- Take advantage of the analytics and predictive capabilities of Power BI
- Make your solutions more dynamic and user specific and/or defined including use cases of parameters, functions, and row level security
- Understand the differences and implications of DirectQuery, Live Connections, and Import-Mode Power BI datasets and how to deploy content to the Power BI Service and schedule refreshes
- Integrate other Microsoft data tools such as Excel and SQL Server Reporting Services into your Power BI solution

Leave a review - let other readers know what you think

Please share your thoughts on this book with others by leaving a review on the site that you bought it from. If you purchased the book from Amazon, please leave us an honest review on this book's Amazon page. This is vital so that other potential readers can see and use your unbiased opinion to make purchasing decisions, we can understand what our customers think about our products, and our authors can see your feedback on the title that they have worked with Packt to create. It will only take a few minutes of your time, but is valuable to other potential customers, our authors, and Packt. Thank you!

Index

www.ingramcontent.com/pod-product-compliance
Lightning Source LLC
Chambersburg PA
CBHW080525060326
40690CB00022B/5031